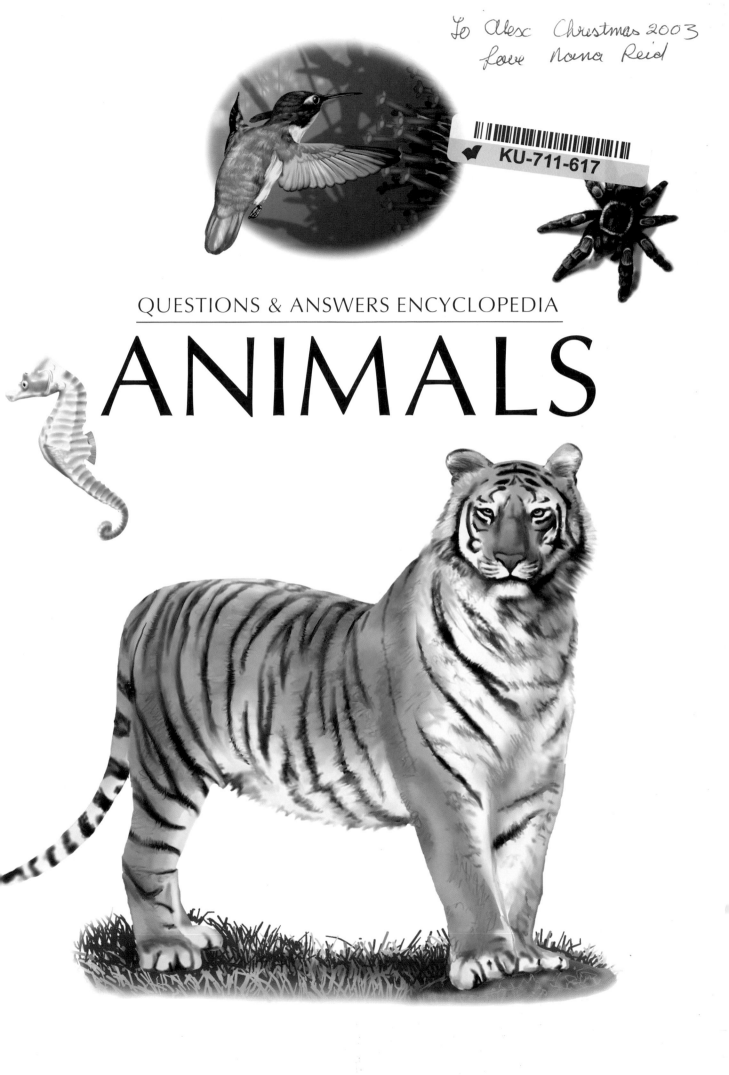

QUESTIONS & ANSWERS ENCYCLOPEDIA

ANIMALS

QUESTIONS & ANSWERS ENCYCLOPEDIA
ANIMALS

This is a Parragon Publishing Book
This edition published 2003
Parragon Publishing
Queen Street House
4 Queen Street
Bath BA1 1HE, UK

Copyright © Parragon 2001

This book was created by Blackjacks Limited

ISBN 0-75259-623-3

Printed in China

Written by Anita Ganeri, Jen Green, Lucinda Hawksley,
Malcolm Penny, Joyce Pope and John Stidworthy.

Illustrated by Michael Posen.

CONTENTS

SECTION ONE

COLD-BLOODED CREATURES

This Nile crocodile has a typically pointed snout.

SO, WHAT IS A REPTILE?

A reptile is an animal that you are most likely to see in the warmer parts of the world. It may be smaller than one of your fingers, or many times bigger than you are. But like you, it will always have a skeleton and it will breathe air. It may be brightly colored or dull shades of brown or grey, but its skin will be hard and dry to the touch.

WHAT DOES COLD-BLOODED MEAN?

Cold-blooded means that an animal does not have a thermostat inside its brain, like we do, to keep its body at the same temperature all the time. Cold-blooded animals like reptiles rely on the sun to heat them up.

DO ALL REPTILES LOOK ALIKE?

No! The slow-moving tortoises and their relatives are shaped like half an orange, and covered in armor made of bone and horn. Crocodiles have sprawly legs and long tails, flattened at the sides. They are armored with little plates of bone. Lizards also have sprawly legs but they have a scaly skin, which is often brightly colored. And, of course, snakes have no legs at all.

HAVE SOME REPTILES GOT THREE EYES?

Not three eyes that can focus and actually see things, but many reptiles have a light-sensitive area in the top of their head, and this is sometimes called a third eye. The "third eye" may act as a short-cut to the brain and some actions that depend on light are probably controlled by it.

HOW OLD DO REPTILES GET?

As a rule, reptiles live longer than mammals or birds of a similar size. Very big reptiles live for much longer than warm-blooded animals and it's likely that a really large crocodile may have passed its 200th birthday. Big tortoises live to a similar age.

WHAT IS THE WORLD'S SMALLEST REPTILE?

The smallest of all reptiles are dwarf geckos, which live in the West Indies. They are less than 2 inches long when fully grown—and over half of this length is tail! Very little is known about these tiny lizards, but like all geckos they feed on insects.

HOW MANY KINDS OF REPTILES ARE THERE?

There are about 6,000 different kinds of reptiles. These can be divided into groups that include around 20 crocodiles and alligators; 600 tortoises, terrapins, and turtles; 2,500 lizards, and a similar number of snakes. One group contains only one animal—a living fossil called the tuatara.

Iguanas belong to the lizard family. This one is sunning itself on a tree branch.

WHEN ARE REPTILES INVISIBLE?

Some reptiles are brightly colored and easy to see. But most are camouflaged with shades of brown, green, and gray, so that they disappear into their background. Often they sit very still and are almost impossible to spot.

ARE REPTILES VERY BRAINY BEASTS?

Compared to mammals, and most of all to ourselves, reptiles are not that smart. They use their instincts for most of the things they do. It's difficult to study the intelligence and behavior of wild reptiles, but pet lizards can recognize their owners by voice and appearance.

WHAT IS THE WORLD'S BIGGEST REPTILE?

The longest reptile is a snake called the reticulated python. It often measures over 18 feet. The heaviest reptile is the saltwater crocodile. An old male may weigh as much as 2,200 lb.

RETICULATED PYTHON

The reticulated python is happy both on land and in water.

Loggerhead turtles are very good swimmers.

LOGGERHEAD TURTLE

HOW DO TURTLES SWIM?

Turtles have webbed feet, which they use like frogman flippers to swim. Sea turtles use their two front feet together and steer with their hind flippers. Although they look ungainly on land, in the water turtles are graceful animals.

CAN REPTILES CLIMB TREES?

Many kinds of lizards live in trees, using their sharp claws to cling on as they climb. Some snakes also live in trees. They wriggle up the tree trunks, holding on with the big scales on their undersides.

Geckos are expert fly catchers.

GECKO

WHAT RUNS UPSIDE-DOWN?

Geckos are lizards that sometimes come into houses and run about on the ceiling. They do this without falling because their toes have little flaps of skin that make their feet into suction pads, which hold them safely.

HOW FAST DOES A SNAKE STRIKE ITS PREY?

A striking prairie rattlesnake moves its head at an average speed of 8 feet per second. But a human's fist punching toward an opponent moves faster.

ARE REPTILES LONG-DISTANCE RUNNERS?

No. Reptiles run out of puff very quickly, so they can't run far. If a reptile has a long distance to travel it will do so slowly, in its own time.

FLYING LIZARD

Flying lizards glide through the air, rather than fly.

HOW DOES A SNAKE MANAGE WITHOUT LEGS?

Snakes generally move by throwing their bodies into big curves and holding against the ground with the scales of their undersides. They must have a rough surface to move over. Put a snake on a piece of glass and it would wriggle about helplessly.

WHAT ARE SIDEWINDERS?

Sidewinders are snakes that live in sandy deserts. They move across the loose surface by looping their bodies up in the air and pushing hard against the ground where they land. The track that a sidewinder leaves in the sand is just a series of straight lines at an angle to the direction in which it is traveling. They show where its body touched down for a moment.

WHERE DO REPTILES MOVE FASTER THAN HUMANS?

It's a close thing! Water reptiles such as turtles or crocodiles can outswim a human easily. On land, a really hungry crocodile could move fast enough to catch a person. Otherwise, humans can outrun most reptiles—except where the ground is very rough. Beware!

CAN REPTILES FLY?

The pterosaurs, which lived at the same time as the dinosaurs, had huge bat-like wings and flew well. Today, the best that a few forest-dwelling reptiles can do is to glide from one tree to another. The champion gliders are little lizards that have long ribs, some of which they fold back against their sides. Leaping from a branch, they spread their ribs, opening umbrella-like fans of skin. Then they glide, like brightly colored paper darts, for up to 60 feet. Some other lizards and a few snakes flatten their bodies as they leap, but they cannot glide far.

WHY DO REPTILES HAVE A CURVY WALK?

Most reptiles have legs that stick out from the sides of their bodies. They always use diagonal limbs (left front foot, right hind foot) together. Because of this, they swing their bodies into a big curve, which makes it easy for them to take a long stride. Even reptiles like snakes and some lizards that have no legs at all, move in a series of curves. Small crocodiles may gallop, but other reptiles never do, even when they are going as fast as they can. However, some lizards can run on their hind legs.

Some lizards can move much faster on hind legs than they can on all fours.

GOULD'S MONSTER

WHERE DO THE BIGGEST REPTILES LIVE?

The leathery turtle lives in the sea. The biggest reptiles of all—crocodiles and the largest snakes—always live near water. Strangely, the biggest land reptiles all live on tiny islands. These include the Komodo dragon, which is the biggest lizard and lives on the island of Komodo, and the giant tortoises of the Galapagos Islands.

ARE REPTILES GOOD AT DIY?

No. Reptiles are not home-makers like many mammals. Some may dig burrows to live in, but more often they find a crack in the rocks or a hole in the ground where they can shelter. A few take advantage of the den-making skills of other creatures. The tuatara lives in a burrow made by a bird and some snakes lodge in prairie dog townships.

HOW DO REPTILES WHILE AWAY THE WINTER?

Without the sun, they slow down, and some of them stop altogether! As the weather gets colder, reptiles move more slowly, eat less, and rest more. In places where winter weather is really harsh, they find safe places to hibernate. Often hundreds of them sleep together through the cold season.

WHERE DO REPTILES LIVE?

Reptiles make their homes in all sorts of places—in deserts and forests, on plains and in water. Sea snakes and sea turtles live in the oceans. Crocodiles are always found near water, but usually the fresh water of rivers and lakes. Many lizards and some snakes are good climbers and hunt for their prey in the branches of trees. Others burrow underground, often to escape from harsh weather. A few geckos and lizards make their homes in human houses. People often welcome them, because they eat insect pests.

HOW DO REPTILES GET TO BE ON REMOTE ISLANDS?

Scientists think that reptiles first got to small islands like Komodo by accident, probably floating on trees that were washed into the sea by big storms. Once they had reached the islands, the reptiles found that they had no enemies. They had no need to hide and in time they became very big.

KOMODO DRAGON

WHICH REPTILES LIKE TO GET IN THE SWIM?

Water is the home for crocodiles and alligators, sea snakes and turtles. Terrapins live in fresh water and some snakes also spend much of their lives near rivers or lakes, though they often come on to dry land. Very few lizards are water-living creatures.

The sea krait uses its curving body to push itself through water.

WHICH REPTILES LIVE IN TREES?

Forests are the home for many kinds of reptile. With their long claws, lizards are good climbers and even snakes squirm their way up trees to hunt birds and insects. Tortoises find shelter on the forest floor and terrapins often live in forest rivers.

ALLIGATOR SNAPPING TURTLE

The alligator snapping turtle can live to over 100 years old.

HOW DO REPTILES HELP US STUDY EVOLUTION?

Scientists compare reptiles that are found on remote islands with their relations on the nearest mainland. They can often discover which sort of reptile reached the island first, because it has had most time to develop and so is least like its mainland cousins.

WHICH REPTILE LIVES AT THE NORTH POLE?

No reptile lives right at the North Pole, but several kinds are found north of the Arctic Circle, where the weather is extremely cold for much of the year. In Europe the adder lives further north than any other reptile. You could find it in the Arctic Circle in northern Sweden and Finland.

When people first saw the Komodo dragon they thought it was a real dragon.

WHICH REPTILES LIKE EATING JELLYFISH?

Almost all marine turtles eat some jellyfish, but the great leathery turtle feeds on little else. It seems strange that this armored reptile, which may weigh up to 1,500 lb and be as long as a tall man, should eat only soft, jellylike creatures.

DO REPTILES CHEW THEIR FOOD?

No, they don't. Reptiles that feed on flesh generally swallow their meals whole, or in very large chunks. Plant-eating reptiles have teeth or jaws that cut their food up, but they don't grind it into small pieces like horses or rabbits do.

HOW OFTEN DO REPTILES EAT?

Reptiles that eat large meals don't need to eat very often. One that has just gorged itself on a huge meal may not eat again for several months. Very big snakes and crocodiles have been known to go for over two years between meals!

DO MOST REPTILES EAT BIG MEALS?

Big reptiles eat big meals for their size. A crocodile may scoff a buffalo or a young giraffe, but a little lizard is content with a few insects.

WHAT REPTILES ARE VEGETARIAN?

The chief plant-eaters among the reptiles are the land tortoises and some lizards. Pet tortoises often eat favorite plants in your garden! The giant tortoises from the Galapagos Islands feed mainly on hard, prickly cacti. Some plant-eating lizards always go for yellow flowers. The strangest plant-eater of all is the marine iguana, which feeds on seaweeds.

DO REPTILES NEED TO DRINK?

All animals need water and reptiles are no exception. Some drink large quantities when water is available and are able to store it in a dry season. Giant snakes that may not eat for a long time still need to drink between meals.

WHAT DO REPTILES EAT?

Antelopes, fish, worms, insects, jellyfish, cacti, and many other kinds of plants! But most reptiles are choosy and most will eat only one main kind of food. A meat-eater would not try chomping on a plant, no matter how hungry it was, though plant-eaters sometimes nibble at insects or worms. Crocodiles, which are the biggest reptiles, catch the biggest meals.

GALAPAGOS TORTOISE

The chameleon is an expert climber.

CHAMELEON

WHICH REPTILES CATCH THEIR FOOD WITH THEIR TONGUES?

Best-known of the tongue-catchers are the chameleons, which stalk insects in bushes and trees. When the chameleon is close enough, it opens its mouth— slowly, slowly—then suddenly shoots out its tongue, sometimes as much as 10 inches, and grabs the insect on its sticky tip in as little as $\frac{1}{25}$ second!

The gila monster is one of only two poisonous lizards.

WHY ARE SOME REPTILES POISONOUS?

Poisonous reptiles usually feed on animals that move faster than they can, so they would probably get away if they were just bitten, but the venom (poison) stops them from escaping. Not all reptiles are poisonous. But two kinds of lizard and about a third of all known snakes have venomous bites.

GILA MONSTER

Crocodile young hatch from their eggs fully formed.

HOW FAST DOES A BABY REPTILE GROW?

In the early days of life most baby reptiles grow quite quickly. Some alligators, which are about 8 inches long at hatching, grow about 12 inches a year for the first three years. After that they slow down, though they carry on growing for many more years.

ARE REPTILES GOOD, CARING PARENTS?

Not usually! Most reptiles don't look after their families at all, so the babies have to fend for themselves. Baby reptiles are like small copies of their parents. Most are born from eggs laid by the mother. They hatch out of the egg fully formed and ready to go. They may be a different color from the adults and often feed on different food for a while, but for a young reptile, independence is the name of the game.

WHAT IS A REPTILE'S EGG LIKE?

Reptiles' eggs are white or dull colored, without a pointed end, like birds' eggs. Some have a hard shell, but many have a papery outer layer. They all have a yellow yolk, which is food for the embryo (developing young), plus a watery white. Some, but not all, have an air sac, which helps the young to breathe as they hatch out.

ARE ANY BABY REPTILES BORN LIKE MAMMALS?

In some geckos and skinks the eggs that the mother holds inside her body are very small. She overcomes this by giving some nourishment to the growing young before they are born. This is almost like the way that baby mammals develop in the womb.

HOW LONG DOES A BABY REPTILE TAKE TO DEVELOP IN THE EGG?

A long time—much longer than birds with eggs of a similar size. The baby tuatara takes the longest time of all reptiles to develop in its egg—up to 14 months! For many reptiles, the length of time in the egg may depend on the temperature—the colder it is the more slowly they develop.

WHICH REPTILE BABIES DON'T HATCH OUT OF EGGS?

All reptiles hatch out of eggs, but some hatch inside their mother's body. Some reptiles, including most of those that live in cold places, and the sea snakes, do not lay their eggs but hold them inside their bodies. Mostly these eggs have very thin shells and eventually the young break through and are born fully formed from their mother's body. She doesn't look after them beyond birth.

DO REPTILE FATHERS EVER HELP TO BRING UP THEIR FAMILIES?

The male mugger, an Indian crocodile, sometimes crushes the eggs that are about to hatch very gently in his mouth, to help his babies into the world. With the female, he then escorts them down to the water. After this he may help to guard them, but does not teach them to care for themselves.

WHEN DO MALE REPTILES GET REALLY ANGRY?

In the breeding season. Male reptiles may fight for territory and sometimes for mates. The most fearsome fighters are the big monitor lizards, which wrestle and tear at each other with their sharp claws. Some snakes twist round each other and sway in a battle—it looks as if they are dancing. The winner probably earns the right to the biggest female and the best place for egg-laying.

HOW DOES A BABY REPTILE GET OUT OF ITS EGG?

Before it hatches, a baby reptile grows a small, sharp bump on the end of its snout. This is called the "egg caruncle." When the little creature needs to break out of the egg, it twists its head from side to side and the caruncle breaks through the shell. Soon after this, the caruncle disappears.

ADDERS

These adders are "dancing" or fighting for a mate.

The coral snake's bright colours warn off predators.

CORAL SNAKE

WHY ARE SOME REPTILES BRIGHT RED AND BLACK?

The venomous lizards and some small poisonous snakes called coral snakes are black and orange or red. This is called warning coloration, for it tells predators that animals with this color are dangerous. Really large poisonous snakes are not brilliantly colored, perhaps because they are not attacked by small predators.

CAN REPTILES SEE IN COLOR LIKE WE CAN?

Reptiles that are active in daylight can probably see much the same colors as we can. Lizards can distinguish red, orange, yellow, yellowish green, blue, and violet. Giant tortoises can see orange, blue, and green and some terrapins are very sensitive to reds. They may even be able to see infra-red, which is invisible to us.

ARE REPTILES SLIMY?

No, reptiles are never slimy. In some cases the skin is rough to touch, but many people are surprised at how beautifully silky the skin of a snake or a lizard can feel. The scales that cover most reptiles have very few glands, like our sweat glands, which is why the skin is dry. The scales help to protect the animal, and the thin skin between them is often folded. When a reptile like a snake eats a huge meal, its skin can bulge as the folds are stretched out.

WHY DO REPTILES CHANGE COLOR?

Reptiles, particularly lizards, can change their colors for many reasons. They tend to be more intensely colored In bright light, and paler in dull light. Often this helps to camouflage the animal. The lizard may also change color when angry or frightened, as changes in color can make it look bigger or fiercer. The most striking color changes are in courtship displays, when male lizards confront mates or rivals.

This anole lizard uses his brightly colored throat fan to attract a mate.

GREEN ANOLE LIZARD

WHY DO SOME SNAKES BORROW DANGEROUS COLORS?

A predator that has had a bad experience with a poisonous snake will probably avoid other snakes with a red and black warning coloration. So a few non-poisonous snakes are also red and black. They have evolved by tricking predators into thinking they are dangerous when they're not.

WHICH REPTILES WEAR ARMOR?

The bodies of tortoises, terrapins, and turtles are encased in bone that forms their protective shell. The shell is made even stronger by a cover of plates of horn. Crocodiles also wear armor, made of little bones called osteoderms, which are set in the skin. This armor protects them against most enemies.

DO REPTILES CHANGE COLOR AS THEY GROW?

Brightly colored reptiles such as lizards and snakes may change color as they grow. This is usually because as they become bigger they begin to live in slightly different places and need to match different backgrounds. The dull browns and grays of turtles and crocodiles remain the same all their life.

WHICH REPTILE HAS AN INVISIBLE SHADOW?

Lichen bark geckos are little lizards that live in Madagascar. They are hard to see as they rest on the trunk of a tree, because they completely match the color of their background. They also have a narrow flap of skin that runs round their body and drapes on to the tree. This hides the animal's shadow, which might be a give-away to hunters.

This gecko is shedding its skin in one large piece.

MARBLED GECKO

HOW DOES A LIZARD SHED ITS SKIN?

Like us, lizards need to shed their skin. But while we lose our skin all the time in minute flakes, lizards shed theirs from time to time in large pieces. Sometimes a lizard will pull a piece of skin off with its teeth, and eat it. Underneath is a bright new skin.

WHY DO SNAKES HAVE FORKED TONGUES?

So they can "taste" their way about the world. As the tongue flickers out of the snake's mouth, it picks up tiny particles of scent left by other animals. Inside the snake's mouth is a pit lined with cells that are very sensitive to smells. The tongue flickers in the air or on to the ground, then is pushed into the pit to test for smells that might lead to food. The deep fork means that the snake can sample a wider track than it could with a simple, undivided tongue.

The fork in the snake's tongue is very sensitive.

WHY DO SNAKES SWALLOW THEIR FOOD WHOLE?

Snakes' teeth are sharply pointed, good for holding food, but no use for cutting it up or chewing it. So when a snake has caught a meal, it has to swallow it in one piece. It may have to unhitch its jaws so that a really big meal can go down. You can tell when a snake has just eaten well because of the bulge in its body.

CAN SNAKES HEAR THROUGH THEIR JAWS?

Snakes have no eardrums, so they can hardly hear any airborne sounds. But they do have an ear bone that connects with the lower jaw, so they can sense vibrations through their jaw from the ground or water. Like other animals, they have an inner ear which is used for balance.

HOW MANY KINDS OF SNAKE ARE THERE?

There are around 2,500 different kinds of snake known in the world today. Most live in warm countries, though you are not likely to see them, since they are generally shy creatures.

WHAT IS A CONSTRICTOR?

A constrictor means a squeezer—it's a snake that squeezes its prey to death. It does this by throwing a loop of its body round the prey. It then squeezes so hard that the prey is soon suffocated, and the snake can swallow its meal.

By stretching its mouth, the boa constrictor can swallow its prey whole.

BOA CONSTRICTOR

WHICH IS THE BIGGEST SNAKE?

The longest of all snakes is the reticulated python from Indonesia. It is often longer than 19 feet, with some running to over 32 feet. The heaviest snake is the anaconda, which is usually shorter than the python, but much stouter. An anaconda measuring only 17 feet weighs as much as a python of 24 feet.

RATTLESNAKE

Rattlesnakes are dangerous to humans only if disturbed.

WHICH IS THE SMALLEST SNAKE?

The smallest snakes are the blind or thread snakes. They are rarely spotted, as they burrow underground. Some are only 6 inches long when fully grown. They normally feed on ants and termites, which they hunt by smell.

HOW DOES A RATTLESNAKE RATTLE?

A rattlesnake's rattle is made of interlocking pieces of hard material like toenails, which tap against each other when the end of the tail is twitched. The rattle grows longer each time the snake sheds its skin, so an old rattlesnake will have a bigger rattle than a young one. The rattle is used to warn off large animals.

CAN SNAKES SHUT THEIR EYES?

A snake has no eyelids, so it can't shut its eyes, even when it's asleep. As it moves about, its eyes are protected by a transparent scale called a brille. Many people think that snakes have an evil stare, but this is simply because they can't blink.

The golden tree snake is one of several flying snakes.

HOW DOES A FLYING SNAKE FLY?

No snake can fly like a bird, but the golden tree snake comes nearest to it. As it launches itself from a branch, it pulls in its belly, so it is concave, like a long wing, and shaped like this it can glide for several feet.

GOLDEN TREE SNAKE

WHICH ANIMAL HAS 45 SETS OF TEETH BEFORE IT IS FULLY GROWN?

Even if it could, a crocodile never has any need to wear false teeth. As the animal grows and its teeth wear down, they are replaced by sharp new ones growing in its jaws. By the time it is a young adult, a Nile crocodile will probably have used up 45 sets of teeth!

WHERE ARE CROCODILES FARMED?

In many parts of the world where crocodiles have become very rare, people are now breeding them in crocodile farms. Some are released into the wild but most are killed and used for leather and for meat.

HOW DO BABY CROCODILES CALL THEIR MUM?

When they are ready to hatch, baby crocodiles croak to their mother from inside the egg. Then she knows it's time to help them hatch. In the water she warns them of danger by twitching her body. The babies feel the water swirling and cluster round her for safety.

WHY IS THE CROCODILE IN DANGER?

Some types of crocodile have become very rare because people have destroyed their habitat. Many other types have been hunted to the brink of extinction. Only now that crocodiles are disappearing have people discovered their importance to the environment.

DO CROCODILES USE BIRDS AS TOOTHBRUSHES?

In a way, yes! The Nile crocodile often rests with its mouth open. Birds venture into its open jaws to pick at bits of meat stuck between the teeth, and perhaps feed on parasites lurking there as well. The birds have to leap out of the way if the crocodile suddenly snaps shut its jaws. By taking flight, they can also warn the crocodile of approaching danger.

WHICH IS THE BIGGEST LIVING CROCODILE?

The saltwater crocodile. The largest one recorded so far is over 23 feet long. Others are said to have grown even bigger—in some cases to over 29 feet long—though no accurate records of these have been kept.

The spur-winged plover picks pieces of meat from between the crocodile's teeth.

BASKING CROCODILE

HOW CAN YOU TELL AN ALLIGATOR FROM A CROCODILE?

Crocodiles have pointy snouts.

By its smile! Alligators and their relatives the caimans are very similar to crocodiles and their cousin the gharial. They are all water-living hunters with long jaws crammed with sharp pointed teeth. The easiest way to tell one from the other is that when an alligator has its mouth closed, you can't see any of its lower teeth. A crocodile shows a big tooth sticking up at either side of its mouth.

WHAT DOES A BABY CROCODILE EAT?

After it has finished eating the yolk from its egg, the baby crocodile starts to catch insects. These are its most important prey until it is about two years old.

Alligators have wide, flat heads and rounded noses.

DO CROCODILES LIKE GETTING WATER UP THEIR NOSES?

No. They prefer calm water to swim in. To swim, a crocodile holds its front feet close to its body and forges forward, using its powerful tail like a paddle. If the water is choppy, the crocodile has to raise its head to stop the water getting up its nose.

Like alligators, caimans have wide, flat heads and rounded noses.

WHICH MOTHER CARRIES ITS BABIES IN ITS FEARSOME MOUTH?

Mother crocodiles help their young by breaking away the hard cap of soil over the nest, and digging down to the eggs. They sometimes break the eggs gently in their mouths to free the babies, which are only about 8 inches long. When the family is complete, the mother either leads them down to the water, or carries them—carefully! —in her mouth. For the first months of their life, she protects them by driving away enemies such as storks or other crocodiles.

Gharials have long, thin snouts that they use for fishing.

WHAT CREATURE BLOWS ITSELF UP LIKE A BALLOON?

Chuckwallas live in North American deserts. If one is attacked it dives into a crevice in the rocks and swallows air, so its body is blown up like a balloon. However hard the predator tries to dislodge it, it is unlikely to succeed, for the chuckwalla is stuck in its crevice and can't be budged.

WHICH LIZARD HAS EATEN PEOPLE?

The biggest of all lizards is called the Komodo dragon. This fearsome creature measures up to 10 feet long and weighs over 330 lb. It normally feeds on carrion (animals it finds already dead), but it has been known to kill and eat humans!

WHY SHOULD YOU AVOID BEING BITTEN BY A BEADED LIZARD?

You can tell a beaded lizard because its scales make it look as though it has been sprinkled all over with beads. But the great difference between beaded lizards and other lizards is that they have a poisonous bite. They eat mainly small helpless creatures, and use the bite for self-defense.

IS IT TRUE THAT LIZARDS NEVER STOP GROWING?

Like all reptiles, lizards grow fast when they are young. After they are big enough to mate, they grow more slowly, but it is likely that they don't ever stop growing completely. Tiny lizards are probably short-lived, but the big ones are almost all very old.

HOW DOES A FRILLED LIZARD SCARE ITS ENEMIES?

The frilled lizard turns on its enemies, opens its mouth wide and at the same time spreads a big ruff of brightly colored skin round its neck. This makes it look much larger and fiercer than it really is. Quite often the bluff works and the lizard escapes with its life.

If its vivid ruff doesn't scare off enemies, the frilled lizard will either run away or run towards its enemies, hissing.

The Californian legless lizard looks more like a snake than a lizard.

WHAT LIZARD FLIES?

Lizards cannot fly like birds, but some forest dwellers can glide for about 65 feet between trees. As they leap from a branch they spread a flap of skin supported by ribs.

CALIFORNIAN LEGLESS LIZARD

WHERE DO LIZARDS LIVE?

There are at least 2,500 different kinds of lizards. Except for Antarctica and some very small islands, they live in almost every country in the world. Most of them are found in warm places, but a few live as far north as the Arctic Circle.

IS IT TRUE THAT SOME LIZARDS HAVE NO LEGS?

Yes, quite a lot of lizards are legless—they wriggle along like snakes. Scientists think that the ancestors of these lizards were burrowing creatures, which wriggled their way through the soil. Their legs were not used for this activity, so gradually grew smaller and eventually disappeared altogether.

WHAT CREATURE SHOOTS BLOOD FROM ITS EYES?

If a horned lizard is attacked, it can increase the blood pressure in veins in its eye sockets until they burst. Blood squirts out in a thin stream, traveling up to 48 inches and splattering the attacker. Predators that get the lizard's blood in their eyes or mouth think it is poisonous and leave the lizard alone.

Horned lizards are decreasing in number, though no one is really sure why.

WHICH LIZARDS HAVE THE BIGGEST STOMACHS?

American horned lizards and the Australian moloch lizard feed on nothing but ants. A single meal may consist of 2,500 ants! Their stomachs have to be much larger than average so they can eat such big meals, and may be up to 13% of their total bulk.

HORNED LIZARD

SECTION TWO

UP IN THE SKY

WHEN IS AN EEL REALLY A BIRD?

When it's an avocet. One old country name for the avocet was "awl," like a cobbler's tool, because of its sharp, curved bill. The old English word for this was pronounced more like "eel." Some birds have more than one name, depending on what people notice most about them. The lapwing, named for the way it flies, is also called "peewit" after its call, and "green plover" because that is what it looks like. In Portugal, where they migrate in winter, lapwings are called "birds of winter."

AVOCET

The avocet sweeps its curved bill backward and forward in the water in search of food.

LIGHTNING BIRD

This lightning bird is carved from soapstone.

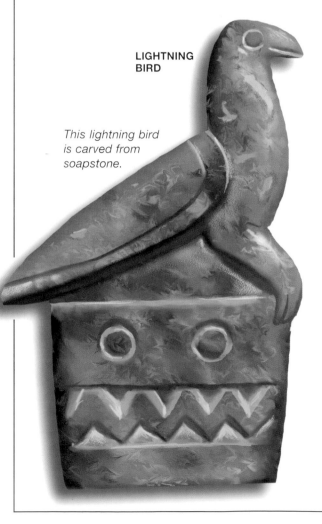

WHY IS A BALD EAGLE CALLED "BALD?"

Because it is piebald, or black and white—not because it doesn't have any hair (or feathers)!

WHAT IS A THUNDERBIRD?

It depends where you are in the world. In ancient Zimbabwe, lightning birds were said to look rather like eagles—they were put up to keep storms away. In North America the Indians call the tiny ruby-throated hummingbird a thunderbird, because it makes miniature thunder noises with its wings as it flies. The Romans thought a woodpecker drumming on the sacred oak (the "thunder tree") would bring rain, and this belief survived in Britain after the Romans had left.

WHY DOESN'T ONE SWALLOW MAKE A SUMMER IN THE UK?

Because although the first swallows usually arrive at the end of March and in early April, they come only in ones and twos: the main migration arrives at the end of April, when summer is really on its way. This saying is not really about birds at all: it means "one piece of good luck doesn't mean that everything will be OK from now on."

WHICH IS THE WISEST BIRD?

The Egyptian god of wisdom was often drawn with the head of a sacred ibis, while in ancient Greece the little owl was dedicated to Athene, the goddess of wisdom. To this day, the scientific name for the little owl is Athene.

CAN WE FORECAST THE WEATHER FROM FEEDING SWIFTS?

Swifts catch insects on the wing, so when the insects are flying high, so do the swifts. Insects fly higher in windier weather, when rain is more likely: so high-feeding swifts may be a sign of rain. On the other hand, insects fly low in humid or thundery weather. Take your pick!

WHY DO PEOPLE SAY THAT A TUMBLING ROOK BRINGS RAIN?

It doesn't, but the weather in Britain is so hard to predict that people will try anything! Rooks perform their tumbling display flights in fall, and it often rains in fall, so the flights are often followed by rain.

CAN BIRDS PREDICT THUNDER?

Country people say that if the dawn chorus is late there will be a storm. This makes sense. The dawn chorus starts at first light, and if heavy clouds make the morning dark, birds will start to sing late, or not at all.

THOTH

The Egyptian god of wisdom, Thoth, had the head of a bird and the body of a man.

Unlike birds today, Archaeopteryx (shown in a fossil here) had teeth.

FOSSILIZED ARCHAEOPTERYX

HOW MANY TOES DO BIRDS HAVE?

Two, three, or four. A typical perching bird has three pointing forward and one back; birds that run on hard ground have only three, all pointing forward. Ostriches have only two toes, shaped rather like the hoof of an antelope. Woodpeckers have two toes pointing forwards and two back; owls can turn their fourth toe either forward or backward, for perching on a branch, or to get a better grip on prey. Swifts have all four toes pointing forwards.

WHY DO BIRDS' KNEES BEND BACKWARD?

They don't. What looks like the bird's knee is in fact its ankle, and below it is an extended foot bone leading to the toes. Its real knee is usually hidden by feathers.

DO BIRDS HAVE FINGERS?

Yes, three of them. The first, the thumb, supports a small but important part of the wing called the alula or bastard wing; the second and third support the main flight feathers.

WHAT IS THE LINK BETWEEN FEATHERS AND DINOSAURS?

Feathers are modified scales, made from a protein called beta-keratin, which is otherwise found only in lizard skin. Birds are descended from ancient lizards related to dinosaurs: the earliest known bird, *Archaeopteryx*, has many reptile-like features.

WHICH BIRD HAS THE LONGEST WINGS?

The wandering albatross has a wingspan—the distance from one wingtip to the other when the wings are stretched out—of more than 10 feet. The longest ever measured was a male with a wingspan of 11 feet; females are usually smaller.

The skeleton of a bird's wing

WHY DO SOME BIRDS HAVE HOOKED BEAKS?

For catching and tearing their prey. Hawks, eagles and, vultures, but also owls and shrikes, need to be able to take a firm grip on struggling prey animals, and then pull them apart to eat them. The edges of an eagle's beak act like a pair of scissors, to cut through skin and flesh. Gulls have a sharp hook at the tip of their bill to hold on to slippery fish or squid.

The sharp, hooked beak of an American bald eagle helps it tear apart its prey.

BALD EAGLE

WHY DON'T BIRDS FALL OFF A BRANCH WHEN THEY GO TO SLEEP?

Tendons from the tips of the toes pass behind the ankle joint. This joint is bent when the bird sits down, so the toes are automatically clenched round the twig it is standing on. No muscle power is involved in this grip, so the bird can sleep without danger of falling.

JACANA

WHICH BIRDS TROT ON LILIES?

Jacanas are sometimes called "lily-trotters." they live on ponds and lakes, walking on lily pads to catch the insects that live on them. Their long toes spread their weight, so that the leaves don't bend and sink.

A jacana walking on lily pads.

WHY ARE BIRD BONES FILLED WITH AIR?

The long bones of birds are like tubes, often with criss-crossing inside, to make them stronger for their weight. Not all birds have equally hollow bones: those that dive into water, like gannets, terns, and kingfishers, and those that fly very fast, like swifts and some waders, have less air in their long bones.

WHICH BIRDS TREAT THEIR NESTS WITH PESTICIDE?

European starlings do. Before the female begins nesting in a hole in a tree, the male bird gathers pieces of green vegetation and puts them into the hole. Scientists have discovered that the male chooses plants that give off certain chemicals which kill parasites, such as bird lice. This helps to keep the nest—and the baby birds that are born in it—free from lice.

WHAT BIRDS LAY THEIR EGGS IN A COMPOST HEAP?

Mound birds in Australia and New Guinea dig large holes in the sandy ground, and lay their eggs on a pile of rotting vegetation they have collected in the bottom. The compost warms the eggs from below, and the sun warms them from above. The parents remove or add sand to keep the temperature constant. After all this work, when the chicks hatch the parents aren't at all interested!

HOW DO BIRDS LEARN TO BUILD NESTS?

They know instinctively what to do and what materials to use, but older birds build better nests than beginners. This suggests that they get better with practice, and also that they know where to find the best materials.

WHICH BIRD LAYS THE WORLD'S SMALLEST EGG?

The smallest is that of the bee hummingbird, which is under ½ x ⅓ inch, and weighs barely anything at all. The egg of the emperor penguin weighs just over one percent of the weight of the female.

HUMMINGBIRD EGG

OSTRICH EGG

From the smallest to the largest—compare the size of an ostrich egg with a hummingbird egg!

WHICH BIRD LAYS A WHOPPER?

The biggest egg is laid by the ostrich: it measures 7 x 5 inches and weighs 3 lb. The biggest egg for the size of the mother is laid by the kiwi, whose eggs, 5 inches long, can weigh as much as 1 lb, a third of the weight of the bird.

QUETZAL

The ancient Aztecs and Mayas worshipped the quetzal bird as the god of the air.

WHICH BIRDS DIG HOLES TO NEST IN?

Many birds dig holes for their nests, including kingfishers and sand martins in sandy banks, and woodpeckers in trees. Puffins clean out disused rabbit burrows, the quetzal in Central America scoops out a large hole in a rotting tree trunk.

WHICH BIRDS MAKE THE BIGGEST NESTS?

Eagles. A bald eagle nest in Ohio, USA, which was used for 35 years, was more than 8 feet across and 12 feet deep, weighing 2 tons. Another in Florida was even bigger: nearly 10 feet wide and more than 20 feet deep.

WHICH BIRDS CAN TIE KNOTS?

Many of the African weaver finches start their spherical hanging nests by tying blades of grass to a twig with neat, strong knots.

WHEN DOES A NEST HAVE A ROOF?

Many small birds, especially in the tropics, build domed nests, with a roof to protect them from rain and sun. The roof might be made of almost anything, from strands of grass in weaver nests to bits of plant tied together with spiders' webs in the nests of sunbirds. In Europe, swallows and long-tailed or penduline tits are the best-known domed nest builders.

WHICH CHICKS CAN'T WAIT TO LEAVE HOME?

Lapwings are a good example of nidifugous (nest-leaving) chicks: they leave the nest as soon as they can all walk, within hours of hatching. Nidicolous (nest-living) chicks stay much longer, in the case of macaws (large parrots) for as long as three months.

Scarlet macaws live in areas like Mexico and Bolivia.

HOW DOES A HUNGRY CHICK GET FED FIRST?

A parent feeds the chick that is asking loudest for food. This usually turns out fairly, because chicks that were fed last time the parent came to the nest are quieter than hungry ones. Black storks just put a pile of fish in the middle of the nest and let the chicks take what they want.

WHEN ARE BABY BIRDS BIGGER THAN THEIR PARENTS?

Shearwater chicks have to be able to survive while their parents fly far out to sea to find food, sometimes for as long as 10 days. They can store fat after a meal to keep them going until the next meal. At the peak of their growth, after about 80 days, they can weigh 12 oz, twice as much as their parents. They are not fed for their last 10 days on the nest, so that they lose enough weight to be able to fly.

WHICH BIRDS DON'T LOOK AFTER THEIR CHICKS?

Mound-building birds like the mallee fowl. They leave their eggs to hatch in a mound of sand, from which the chicks eventually scramble out. If the parents see the chicks, they do not even recognize them.

WHY IS IT A GOOD IDEA TO HATCH FIRST?

A partridge might take three weeks to lay 15 eggs, only incubating them when the last is laid, so that they all hatch together. Owls, eagles, herons, and gulls on the other hand, incubate their eggs as soon as the first one is laid, so that the chicks hatch at different times. If food is short, the last chicks to hatch will die.

This lesser whitethroat is feeding a cuckoo chick that hatched in its nest.

WHAT IS AN EGG-TOOTH?

The hardened tip of the chick's beak is called an egg-tooth. It is used to break the first hole in the eggshell just before it hatches.

WHAT IS PIGEON MILK?

This is a fluid rich in protein produced by cells lining the crop of male and female pigeons, used to feed the chicks. Flamingos feed their chicks in the same way: so do emperor penguins, but only the males produce the milk.

DO CHICKS EAT THE SAME AS THEIR PARENTS?

Some do, like chicks of seabirds, which eat fish. But chicks of seed-eating birds usually start life eating insects, because they need the special fats and protein that seeds can't provide. Cuckoo chicks eat whatever their foster-brothers and sisters eat, only much more of it.

CUCKOO

**COUNT RAGGI'S
BIRD OF PARADISE**

WHEN IS PREENING JUST FOR SHOW?

All birds have to preen themselves, but some species of duck go through the motions in a special way as part of their display. The bill never actually touches the feathers, but the bird raises its wing to show off the bright patch of color that is the badge of its species.

Count Raggi's red-plumed bird of paradise uses its stunning red tail feathers to attract mates.

WHY DO BIRDS SHOW OFF?

For much the same reasons as they sing, but with more emphasis on finding and keeping a mate. Males may display (the technical term for showing off) and even fight while the females watch. Ruffs and capercaillie perform a mass display called a lek. Afterwards, the females choose the most successful males to breed with. The most elaborate displays are seen among birds of paradise and peacocks.

Male frigate birds attract a mate with their throat-pouch.

WHEN DOES A FRIGATE BIRD BLOW UP?

Male frigates have a huge red throat-pouch which they inflate to attract females, making a wavering, fluting call as they do so.

FRIGATE BIRD

WHY DO BIRDS SING?

Birds do not sing because they are happy! The two main reasons are to attract a mate and to defend a territory. Birds recognize the song of their own species: females are attracted to a male with a powerful and complex song, and other males are driven away from his territory.

The woodcock is known for it beautiful trilling courtship songs.

WHICH BIRD RAISES A FALSE ALARM?

There can be more to alarm calls than just warning other birds of danger. In the Amazon, when several different species are feeding together in a flock, the white-winged shrike tanager gives an alarm call when it sees another bird find a tasty insect. All the birds fly away in fright—except the crafty tanager, which dashes in and grabs the prey.

WHY DO BIRDS SING OTHER BIRDS' SONGS?

Indian hill mynas are well known for imitating human voices, though they rarely mimic other birds in the wild. But marsh warblers include quotations from hundreds of other species in their song, from both Europe and Africa. This may be because males with more complex songs win more mates. Male mocking birds in America copy the song of another species when it approaches their territory, possibly to drive it away.

DO BIRDS HAVE SINGING LESSONS?

Yes. In a famous experiment with chaffinches, scientists found that young males cannot develop the full song of the species without hearing adult males (or at least recordings of them) singing nearby and copying them.

WHY DO BIRDS PREEN EACH OTHER?

Mutual preening helps to remove parasites such as ticks from places that a bird cannot reach for itself round its head and neck. Since the only birds that do this are the two members of a breeding pair, it is usually seen as part of the "bonding" process that keeps them together.

WOODCOCK

WHY DO GEESE FLY IN A V?

When a bird is flying, the air just behind its wingtips swirls upward. If another bird flies in this turbulent, rising air, it can save about 15% of the energy it would have to use if it were flying alone. In a V-formation, the leader is the only bird not saving energy: other birds take its place from time to time, to share the burden of leadership. Swans and cranes are among other birds that use this technique.

WHAT IS THE SLOWEST BIRD IN THE WORLD?

Surprisingly, swifts are among the slowest-flying birds, moving at less than 12 mph while they are feeding. Their insect prey moves only slowly, so they must move slowly to gather it. They fly faster than this at other times, as they wheel and swoop close to buildings and people. Another answer to this question could be hummingbirds, because when they hover they move at 0 mph! Even better, they are the only birds that can fly backward under power, registering a negative speed!

WHAT KEEPS A BIRD UP IN THE AIR?

The shape of its wings. The upper surface is raised in a curve, so that air travel ing across it has to move faster than air moving under the wing. Air moving faster is at a lower pressure than slower air, so the higher pressure under the wing pushes it upwards as it moves through the air. The first humans to discover how this "aerofoil section" works were Australian Aborigines, when they invented the boomerang.

HOW DO BIRDS LAND?

Ideally, by stalling (ceasing to move forward) just as they touch down. Large water birds, like swans, can water-ski to a halt on outstretched feet. Boobies and albatrosses, which spend most of the year at sea, often crash and tumble over when they finally return to land to breed.

WHAT BIRD CAN FLY FOR SIX HOURS WITHOUT MOVING ITS WINGS?

With its long, narrow wings, an albatross is perfectly adapted for gliding, even in still air. But when it glides close to the sea surface it can make use of wind currents from the waves, giving it an almost continuous source of lift, meaning that in this type of flight it only has to hold its wings still.

BLACK BROWED ALBATROSS

The albatross can soar for as long as six hours without moving its wings.

The bee hummingbird hovers as it feeds from a flower.

BEE HUMMINGBIRD

HOW DOES A HUMMINGBIRD HOVER?

By keeping its body nearly vertical while its wings beat forward and backward. It is actually flying upward just fast enough to balance its body weight, so that it stays still. A ruby-throated hummingbird, which weighs less than ⅛ oz has to beat its wings more than 52 times a second to hover in front of a flower.

WHAT IS THE WORLD'S FASTEST BIRD?

People will always argue about this. Most think that the peregrine falcon is the fastest bird by far, but when its speed was accurately measured the maximum in level flight was 58 mph. Measurements by radar show that eider ducks fly for long periods at 45 mph, but the world record is held by the Asian spine-tailed swift, which has been timed at 102 mph in level flight.

WHAT IS THE HEAVIEST BIRD IN THE AIR?

The Kori bustard, from East and South Africa, weighs about 31 lb: the largest specimen known weighed just over 18 40 lb. Because it finds flying such hard work, the Kori bustard flies only in emergencies, and only for short distances.

WHAT HAS WING SHAPE TO DO WITH FLIGHT?

Birds' wings are shaped differently depending on how they need to fly. Fast flight demands narrow wings, like those of swallows, while quick flight in woodland needs short, rounded wings, like those of a bluetit. Falcons change the shape of their wings from long and narrow for fast flight, to swept-back for diving at top speed. Gannets have long wings for long-distance flight and gliding: when they dive to catch fish they fold their stretched wings backward, like the flights of a dart.

WHICH BIRD SPENDS ITS WHOLE LIFE IN THE SUMMER?

The Arctic tern breeds in the Arctic, to within 430 miles of the North Pole, and migrates every year to the Antarctic, a total distance of 23,000 miles between breeding seasons. It spends its whole life in the summer.

WHY DO SOME BIRDS STAY BEHIND?

In Sweden, female and young chaffinches migrate south in winter, but some males stay behind in their breeding territories. European blackbirds do the same: it seems that the males that stay behind through the winter can hold on to the best breeding territories for when the females return in spring.

WHICH IS THE SMALLEST MIGRANT BIRD?

The rufous hummingbird, less than 4 in) long, flies every year from Alaska to its winter quarters in Mexico, a round trip of 3,800 miles.

HOW FAST DO MIGRATING BIRDS FLY?

Studies using radar show that small birds like warblers move at about 21 mph when they are migrating, and ducks at about 42 mph. They usually fly for only about six or eight hours a day, but one knot ringed in England was found in Liberia, 3,400 miles away, only eight days later. It had covered an average distance of 420 miles per day; since knots fly at about the same speed as ducks, it must have been traveling for 10 hours every day.

Pigeons are strong-flying birds and good navigators.

PIGEONS

WHERE DID PEOPLE THINK SWALLOWS WENT IN WINTER?

SWALLOWS

They thought that they hibernated, perhaps in hollow trees, or even in the mud at the bottom of ponds. This is not as crazy as it sounds: in cold weather swallows often roost in groups in hollow trees or chimneys, and in spring they can be seen collecting mud at the edge of pools to make their nests.

Swallows leave cooler countries, such as northern Europe, at the end of summer in search of warmer weather.

WHY ARE LIGHTHOUSES DANGEROUS?

The beams from lighthouses attract migrating birds, especially during misty conditions. Many birds are killed when they fly against the glass.

WHEN DO BIRDS BEHAVE LIKE SAILORS?

When birds migrate, they use a mixture of signs, including the position of the sun and stars for navigating on long-distance flights. They also use local landmarks when they are near their destination. They have a "compass" in their heads with which they can sense the earth's magnetic field, and choose their direction accordingly.

WHY DO MIGRATING BIRDS FLY SO FAR?

To move out of areas which are suitable for breeding back to places where they can survive the winter. The reason for moving back to the breeding area is usually because it contains plenty of food in the summer to feed the chicks.

HOW DO JAYS AND OAK TREES HELP EACH OTHER?

As well as preying on the chicks of other birds, jays feed on acorns. In fall, when acorns are plentiful, jays bury some of them to dig up later. Those that they don't find will grow into new oak trees.

JAY

Jays are very noisy birds. They have harsh, raspy voices.

WHEN IS A THRUSH LIKE A BLACKSMITH?

A song thrush uses a stone, called an anvil, to kill snails, which it beats against the stone until the shell breaks.

WHICH BIRD EATS ONLY SNAILS?

The Everglades kite, in Florida, is a genuine bird of prey, with strong talons and a sharply hooked beak, but its only food is apple snails. As the Everglades dry up, the snails are becoming scarce, which is why the kite is also becoming rare.

WHY DON'T WOODPECKERS GET HEADACHES?

When a woodpecker drills the bark of a tree, using its head as a hammer and its beak as a chisel, soft, spongy bone between the beak and the skull absorbs most of the impact.

WHY ARE HUMMINGBIRDS GOOD FOR FLOWERS?

They pollinate them when they collect nectar. Grains of pollen stick to the hummingbird's head, and are transferred to the next flower it visits.

DO BIRDS USE TOOLS?

Yes. Woodpecker finches in the Galapagos use cactus spines to winkle out larvae from their burrows in dead wood, because they can't reach them with their short beaks. Egyptian vultures pick up stones and drop them on ostrich eggs to break them. Green-backed herons in the United States have been seen using bread as bait to bring fish within reach of their bill.

WHY DO GANNETS END UP IN FISHING NETS?

People used to say that gannets can dive to 164 feet, because they are sometimes found caught in fishing nets set at that depth. But they stay underwater for 10 seconds or less, so they wouldn't have time to get that deep. In fact, they rarely dive more than 32 feet: the unfortunate birds in the nets must have been caught and killed as the nets were pulled up.

HOW DO BIRDS CATCH FISH?

With their beaks—which often have a hooked tip or jagged edges to help them grip their prey—or with their feet, like fish eagles or ospreys. As well as long, curved talons, the feet often have roughened soles to improve the grip. The African fish eagle strikes its prey with its long hind talon and then clenches the others round it.

Gannets swim under water using their feet and half-opened wings.

This African fish eagle is just about to strike its prey.

AFRICAN FISH EAGLE

HOW MANY KINDS OF BIRD HAVE BECOME EXTINCT?

More than 150 since 1600—that we know about—and probably many more that no one ever noticed. It wasn't just European explorers who did the damage: archaeology shows that when people first arrived in ancient times on Hawaii, and islands in the South Pacific and the Caribbean, they killed many birds that Europeans never even saw.

WHY IS IT DANGEROUS FOR BIRDS TO LIVE ON ISLANDS?

Until humans came along, islands were among the safest places for birds to live, but people soon changed that. The first danger came from passing sailors, who came ashore for water and wood, and without knowing it brought rats with them. Rats are very good predators on island birds. When people started to live in the islands, cats and dogs, and even pigs, continued the damage started by the rats.

WHO ATE THE DODO AND THE SOLITAIRE?

The dodo was a large, flightless pigeon living on Mauritius. All dodos were wiped out when people first came to their islands. Some were eaten by people, and the rest by introduced pigs and rats. By the middle of the 18th century they were all extinct.

DODO

Dodos were land birds with thick, heavy feathers.

WHO IS DESTROYING THE WORLD'S FORESTS?

The increasing human population. In the tropics, people clear forests to grow food for their families or for large companies. The demand for large timber in Europe, North America, and Japan is all too often met by chopping down irreplaceable ancient forests.

WHY IS THE NÉNÉ IMPORTANT?

The néné was the first bird species to be bred in captivity—at the Wildfowl and Wetlands Trust in England and in Hawaii—with the intention of releasing it back into its home when it was safe to do so. The operation was a success.

NÉNÉ

The néné, also called the Hawaiian goose, has been saved from extinction by being bred in captivity.

WHERE IS THE ENDANGERED BARN OWL A PEST?

In the Seychelles, where someone had the bright idea of introducing barn owls from South Africa to kill rats. They instantly started killing birds instead, especially fairy terns, and taking over the nest sites of the rare Seychelles kestrel.

WHY WAS NORTH AMERICA'S COMMONEST BIRD MADE EXTINCT?

Before 1840 there were thousands of millions of passenger pigeons in North America, but they were slaughtered for food until only one was left—a female called Martha—who died at 12 years old in 1914, in a zoo in Ohio.

HOW MANY OF THE WORLD'S BIRD SPECIES ARE ENDANGERED?

Eleven percent, most of them because of the harm done by people to the natural environment. Draining wetlands and felling forests are the main causes of damage, but the misuse of pesticides and industrial pollution also play a part.

WHY DOES THE CALIFORNIAN CONDOR OWE ITS SURVIVAL TO A GLOVE PUPPET ?

When condors, nearly extinct in the wild, were being bred in captivity, scientists wanted to avoid the chicks becoming too familiar with humans. They fed them with meat held in a glove puppet that looked like a condor's head.

SECTION THREE

CREEPY CRAWLIES

CRAB SPIDER

CAN SPIDERS CHANGE COLOR?

The crab spiders, such as *Misumena*, live in flowers. They lie in wait for insects, sitting on flowers whose colors they match. They are even capable of changing color over a few days to match the flower. Most kinds of spider stay the same color, but their natural coloring or pattern is often perfect camouflage for their habitat.

WHICH ARE THE BIGGEST SPIDERS?

The "bird-eating" spiders of South America are both the heaviest and widest species, with weights up to 3 oz and leg spans up to 10 inches. Very few of them actually eat birds, but the bigger species do eat small frogs, lizards, and snakes.

HOW MANY KINDS OF SPIDER ARE THERE?

There are over 30,000 species discovered so far, but there could be as many again that haven't yet been found. Spiders can live virtually all over the world on land.

DO ALL SPIDERS HAVE WEBS?

Not all spiders make a nice round web. Some weave hammock-shaped webs, flat sheets of silk or simply trip wires radiating from their lair to trap insects. Some hunt without using a web, but all spiders can make silk.

ARE SPIDERS GOOD PARENTS?

Most spiders don't really look after their young. Many lay their eggs in a cocoon for protection, but often the female will die before they hatch. Mother wolf spiders carry the cocoon attached to their spinnerets (the organ that makes their silk), and *Pisaura* carries her cocoon in her fangs until hatching time, when she builds a silk tent on a plant for the babies to live in. The tiny *Theridion sisyphium* lives in a thimble-shaped tent above its hammock web. In the tent it looks after the egg cocoon, then feeds the tiny babies below it with the regurgitated juices from the prey.

RED-KNEED TARANTULA

The largest spiders, like this red-kneed tarantula, are little danger to humans.

WHICH SPIDERS GIVE PRESENTS?

Male spiders are often smaller than their mates. Sometimes the female may attack the male in order to eat him. Many American wolf spiders "sing" to the female to distract her and try and save themselves. The male spider *Pisaura mirabilis* of Europe makes himself safe by catching a fly, wrapping it into a silk parcel, and presenting it to the female, who eats it as they mate. He does this in the hope that she won't be hungry enough to make a meal of him.

TRAPDOOR SPIDER

WHICH SPIDERS ARE HUMAN KILLERS?

All spiders are poisonous, but only a few have strong enough fangs and venom to harm people. The black widow, found in many warm parts of the world is a small, round spider which likes hiding in quiet places. It is not aggressive, but if it is attacked, it may bite. After a few minutes, the bite is terribly painful. The victim feels dizzy and can suffer from paralysis. It is rarely fatal, though, and nowadays cures are available. The Australian Sydney funnel-web spider is a larger species with a bite that causes heart failure and breathing problems. The recluse spiders of the USA and the Brazilian wandering spider also have bites that can be fatal. However, the chances of being killed by a spider are less than those of being struck by lightning.

The small and shiny black widow spider can inject a venom more powerful than that of many rattlesnakes.

WHICH SPIDER MAKES THE BIGGEST WEBS?

The tropical orb web spiders can have webs over 16 feet across. Up to 2,300 feet length of silk strand can be produced by the silk glands of one of these spiders. The silk is so strong it can actually hold a human.

WHAT IS A SPIDER'S WEB MADE OF?

A spider's web is made of silk. Spiders have glands on their abdomen which produce the silk, which can be made sticky, elastic, or very strong. Some spider silk is much stronger than steel of the same thickness.

HOW MANY EYES DOES A SPIDER HAVE?

Most spiders have eight eyes, but there are species with six, four, or two. The shape and arrangement of the eyes help to tell the family a spider belongs to. Many spiders use touch more than sight, but the eyes of jumping spiders are well developed.

WHICH CREEPY-CRAWLY LIVES UNDER A TRAPDOOR?

Trapdoor spiders dig a burrow in the forest floor and cover it with an earth trapdoor. The spider lurks in its burrow, the door half-open, until something tasty to eat walks by. Then it pounces, drags the prey underground, and slams the trapdoor shut.

CAN SPIDERS FLY?

Spiders do not have wings, but many species can parachute or sail through the air by letting out a long thread of silk until they are carried away by the wind. Many young spiders leave the nest by this "ballooning" technique. They can be carried thousands of feet above the earth.

Trapdoor spiders come from Central America.

DO ALL SCORPIONS STING?

All scorpions have poisonous stings at the ends of their tails. They use them mainly to defend themselves. Only a few are truly dangerous to humans. Most scorpion stings are unpleasant rather than deadly.

WHEN DO SCORPIONS DANCE?

The mating ritual of scorpions looks like a dance. The partners grab one another's pincers, to protect themselves from each other. With pincers held, they move back, forward, and sideways, sometimes for hours. Finally, the male deposits a packet of sperm and moves the female over the top of it. The sperm goes into her body and fertilizes the eggs.

Scorpions first appeared on Earth 345 million years ago.

WHERE DO BABY SCORPIONS HITCH A RIDE?

After hatching, the young of many scorpions climb onto their mother's back. They use her large pincers as a climbing ramp. They ride there until after their first moult (when they lose a layer of skin). After this they leave their mother and start to fend for themselves.

WHERE DO THE BIGGEST SCORPIONS LIVE?

The largest scorpions live in tropical forests. Some, such as the imperial scorpion of Africa, are up to 7 in long. These scorpions aren't very poisonous.

IMPERIAL SCORPION

HOW BIG ARE THE BIGGEST MILLIPEDES?

Some of the millipedes that live in the tropical parts of Africa grow to 11 inches or more, with a diameter (thickness) of about 1 inch.

HOW MANY LEGS DOES A MILLIPEDE REALLY HAVE?

In spite of their name (*mille* is Latin for a thousand), millipedes never have a thousand legs. The most that they have is 200 pairs (400 legs), and some species have only 20 pairs (40 legs). The leg movements are co-ordinated in "waves" running from front to back.

Millipedes have two pairs of legs in each segment of their bodies, while centipedes have just one pair per segment.

HOW CAN YOU TELL A MILLIPEDE FROM A CENTIPEDE?

Most millipedes are slow-moving plant-eaters with short legs and chewing mouthparts. Centipedes are fast-moving meat-eaters with fangs that they use to kill prey. They have fewer legs than millipedes.

GIANT MILLIPEDE

WHAT TICK CARRIES A MOUNTAINOUS DISEASE?

A serious illness, called Rocky Mountain fever, is caused by a tiny organism called a rickettsia. It invades the cells of the body and produces severe fever. The disease is carried by woodchucks, but wood ticks, living on these animals, can carry it to humans. The disease was first discovered in Montana about 100 years ago, when it killed three-quarters of those who got it. Since then, it has been found in other parts of North and South America, but not in such a deadly form.

WILL YOU EVER BE ATTACKED BY A CENTIPEDE?

Centipedes have a pair of poison fangs that they use to catch their prey. Most centipedes in countries with a mild climate do not have a powerful enough bite to do serious damage. Anyway, they usually run away rather than attack. But some large tropical centipedes can inflict a nasty bite if threatened.

WHY DO TICKS DRINK BLOOD?

Ticks don't find food very often, and they must be ready to latch on to anything that can provide it as it passes. An adult tick may have to wait months or even years before fastening its jaws into a passing mammal and sucking its blood. It has to have a meal of blood before it can lay its eggs.

WHAT INSECT IS MAKING A MEAL OF YOUR SKIN?

A large part of house dust is made up of tiny flakes of human skin and this is what the house dust mite eats. It likes warm, damp conditions, such as in beds and mattresses, which can also provide plenty of skin. Although most people are not affected by these mites, some people are highly allergic to them.

WHAT IS THE BIGGEST EARTHWORM?

The biggest earthworm ever measured was 22 feet long when moving (that's twice the length of a tiger). Most earthworms are under 12 inches long, but the South African worm *Microchaetus* grows to over 3 feet 3 inches. Giant earthworms measure 10 feet. They live in Australia and in Oregon and Washington, USA.

EARTHWORM

WHERE DO KILLER WORMS LIVE?

When humans transport insects to different countries, the effects can be terrible on the species already living in that country. A New Zealand flatworm, called *Artioposthia*, caused havoc when it arrived in the British Isles. It grows to up to 8 inches long, and hunts for earthworms in the top 12 inches of soil. It has greatly reduced earthworm numbers in places where it has spread. In Northern Ireland, some pastures have been totally cleared of earthworms by the invader.

HOW LONG DOES AN EARTHWORM LIVE?

So many earthworms are eaten by birds and animals, from moles to foxes, that the average lifespan of an earthworm is probably very short. However, some have been known to live 10 years.

HOW MANY WORMS ARE THERE IN A BUCKET OF SOIL?

In soil from a fertile meadow, there may be as many as 60 earthworms under each square foot. An average bucket of such soil might contain up to 200. Earthworms play a huge part in turning soil over. This puts air back into it and returns the goodness to it.

Earthworms are very important for keeping soil fertile.

WHICH WORMS CAN YOU CATCH FROM A DOG?

Dogs often have parasitic worms inside them. These can include a tiny tapeworm called *Echinococcus*. The larva forms a cyst the size of an orange inside the host animal. The worm's eggs are passed out in dog feces. A dog that has licked itself clean may have eggs on its tongue. If it licks the face or hand of a human, they may be infected. A huge cyst can form in their body, or most deadly of all, in the brain.

HOW LONG IS A TAPEWORM?

Many kinds of tapeworm infect the gut of animals. In man, the pork tapeworm can grow to 5 feet, but a tapeworm caught from the fish *Diphyllobothrium* can be over 59 feet long.

WHICH WORM LIVES INSIDE PEOPLE?

The human blood fluke is the "flatworm" that causes the disease bilharzia, which attacks millions of people in the Middle East and Africa. The larvae of the worms are released into the water, and burrow into the skin of humans who are wading through the water. Pairs of flukes then live in veins in the gut. Their eggs are passed out through the person's bladder, damaging it as they go.

The leech's body fills with blood as its jaws cut into the human's skin.

LEECH

WHICH WORM SUCKS BLOOD?

The medicinal leech sucks blood from mammals, including humans. In the past, people treated many diseases by "bleeding" the patient. They believed that diseases were caused by too much blood in the body. The leech would use its three teeth to open a wound; its digestive juices anaesthetized wounds and kept blood flowing.

Two gray slugs mate in a slimy embrace, hanging above the ground.

GREAT GRAY SLUGS

WHERE DO SLUGS HANG OUT IN DRY WEATHER?

We always see slugs in wet weather, but where do they go when it dries up? Unlike a snail, a slug cannot hide out in its shell during drought. Many slugs simply burrow deep into the earth and stay there until it is wet again.

DO SLUGS AND SNAILS HAVE TEETH?

Not really. Snails and slugs have no jaws like ours, but they have special ribbon-shaped tongues which are covered in row upon row of horny "teeth." They rasp away at their food and break it into tiny pieces. On a quiet night in the garden, you can hear the noise of snail and slug tongues shredding their food with their file-like tongues.

DO ALL SLUGS EAT PLANTS?

Most slugs are plant-eaters. Some are pests because they attack our crops, but many prefer to feed on dead or decaying plant matter. Shelled slugs, such as *Testacella*, are unusual because they have a tiny bit of shell left on their backs. They are unusual in another way too; they are meat-eaters. They go underground and chase worms. They harpoon them with their tongues, then suck them into their mouths.

WHICH IS THE WORLD'S FASTEST SNAIL?

Most snails are so slow-moving that nobody has bothered to measure their speed, but the fastest snail on record was an ordinary garden snail *Helix aspersa*. This could move at 0.03 mph.

HOW DO SNAILS BREATHE?

Slugs and snails have turned the wall of the mantle (the skin of the snail) into a kind of lung. It is well supplied with blood vessels and encloses a cavity that is full of air. This connects to the outside air through a special hole that can be opened and closed. You can often see this hole on the right of the body if you look at a slug or snail when it's stretched out.

WHICH SLUGS MATE IN MID-AIR?

Most slugs and snails are both male and female in the same body. Even so, they usually mate with another slug or snail, and mating rituals may be very complicated. For example, one great gray slug meets another on the ground and starts a slimy embrace. The pair climb up vegetation, entwining and producing so much slime that it forms a rope up to 39 inches long. The pair dangle from the end of this as they complete their mating in mid-air.

HOW DO SNAILS MOVE WITHOUT LEGS?

Snails move on a single thick pad of muscle known as the "foot." Waves of muscle power move down the underside of the foot, lifting sections and moving them forward, as others are put down. From above the snail appears to glide along. The mucus, or slime, that the snail produces, helps smooth its path, and is sticky enough to help it grip when it climbs.

DO ALL SNAIL SHELLS COIL THE SAME WAY?

In most snails, the shells spiral to the right. If you hold the shell so the mouth is facing you, the mouth is on the right. Some species have a left-handed shell. In each species, all the individuals coil in the same direction.

WHAT DO SNAIL EGGS LOOK LIKE?

Some species produce clutches of up to 100, others fewer. In many cases, they are round and transparent, but other species such as the giant African snail have eggs with a hard chalky shell. The eggs are the size of a small bird's egg.

HOW BIG IS THE BIGGEST SNAIL?

The shell of the giant African snail *Achatina* can be up to 13 inches long. That is as long as a rabbit. The extended snail is longer. A captive specimen was once measured at 15 inches from head to tail, with a shell 10 inches long, and a weight of 32 oz.

WHAT ARE THE RAREST SNAILS IN THE WORLD?

The *Partula* snails of some South Pacific islands may be the rarest in the world, but they are fighting for survival. Giant African snails were introduced to the islands accidentally, but became a farm pest. So, a meat-eating snail was introduced to control them, but preferred to catch the smaller *Partula* snails which are ¾ inch long. The species is now rare, and it is threatened by habitat loss too, but *Partula* snails are being bred in captivity now to try and save them.

HOW DO SNAILS MAKE SHELLS?

The mantle is a skin that covers the parts of the snail that stay within the shell. The shell substance is produced by the edge of the mantle. The shell has a horny layer, then an inner, strengthening layer of calcium carbonate. This is the same chemical as chalk.

Away from its native land, the giant snail has become a giant pest.

GIANT AFRICAN SNAIL

ARE ALL ANTS SOCIABLE?

All ant species are social animals. This means that they live in groups and each of them is given a job to do in the colony. Each colony has at least one egg-laying female, or queen, but she is vastly outnumbered by the ants we usually see, the workers. They are wingless and sterile females—never males.

LEAF-CUTTER ANT

Leaf-cutter ants carry huge pieces of leaf back to their gardens.

WHICH ANTS LIKE A THORNY HOME?

The acacia ant makes its small nest just in the spiny tips of twigs of acacia thorn trees in the savanna (dry plains with bushes and trees). The ants get some protection from the thorns, and they keep the tree free of other harmful insects by eating them.

WHY DO ANTS NEED SLAVES?

Some ants are forced to act as workers for other species. The slave-maker ant of Europe raids the nests of other species and carries the young back to their own nest. When they hatch out, these new workers act as slaves collecting food, feeding other ants and cleaning the nest. Slavery is used by a few ant species.

WHY DO ANTS TAP?

When ants tap each other's antennae, it is a way of communicating. Strong tapping can be a signal of alarm, but in many species, gentle tapping between two ants is a signal for one to give food to the other.

WHY DO ANTS HAVE WINGS?

Ants' wings are only used when they mate. Only fully-grown males and females have wings. Workers do not need them. When they land from their mating flights, females that have been fertilized lose their wings, in some cases chewing them off. They then look for a place to start a new colony and have their young.

SOLDIER ANTS

WHICH ANTS LOOK AFTER "COWS?"

Several kinds of ant feed on a sweet substance, called honeydew, which is produced by aphids (a small bug, such as a greenfly). Some, like the black garden ant, look after herds of aphid "cows" or females, protecting them from predators and even moving them to new plants on which to feed.

HOW DO ANTS KNOW EACH OTHER?

Ants probably don't recognize each other as individuals. But each species has its own chemical messengers, and there may be slight differences between nests too. An ant can recognize another as a nest mate or a stranger by its smell. Chemicals allow the ants to leave scent trails that can be followed by others to good food sources.

A column of marching soldier ants is one of the best killing machines in the animal kingdom.

HOW MANY ANTS ARE THERE IN AN ANT NEST?

Some estimates put the number of ants in such a nest as high as 7 million. Other species have smaller nests, with numbers ranging from thousands to hundreds. The biggest ant nests are those made by the leaf-cutter ants, some of which travel for 33 feet or more underground.

HOW DO ANTS GROW MUSHROOMS?

The leaf-cutter ants of tropical America cut out pieces of leaf to take back to their nest and use as a kind of "manure." Back in their nests, underground, they chew the leaves and add them to their "garden." A fungus grows in this garden (each ant species has its own) which makes a nutritious food.

HOW DO ANTS DEFEND THEIR NESTS?

Many kinds of ant are armed with stings for protection. Others, such as the big wood ant of Europe, can squirt formic acid at enemies. Species with large soldier ants may rely on their jaws to attack invaders. Some species have more specialized ways of keeping trouble out, such as soldiers that block the entrance to the nest with their body.

WHAT SORT OF HOME DOES A WASP HAVE?

A wasp's nest is made of tough paper, known as carton. The wasps tear wood fibers from trees, posts, and fences and chew them to make this paper. It is carefully molded into shape and then inside it is shaped into six-sided cells that the queen lays her eggs in. The nest may be underground or hanging from a tree.

POTTER WASP

This solitary wasp sticks sand grains together to build a flask-shaped nest.

ARE WASPS ANY USE?

Many people think that the yellow and black striped wasps are our enemies. These wasps do have a powerful sting, but it is not often used against humans. In fact, they do an enormous amount of good for people, as they collect a lot of caterpillars and insect grubs, many of which are pests. These are taken back to the nest and chewed up as food for the larvae.

HOW MANY KINDS OF WASP ARE THERE?

There are a surprising number of different kinds of wasp, more than 200,000. Most of them are not the familiar striped social wasps, but are types such as sawflies, wood wasps, sand wasps, and other kinds of hunting wasp.

WHERE DO WASPS GO IN THE WINTER?

Unlike honeybees, wasps do not store up sweet substances in their nests, so the colony has nothing to survive on in the winter. At the end of the summer, after the new queens have mated, the workers all die. Just the queen survives the winter in hibernation, and she starts a new colony in the spring.

WHICH WASP EATS ITS VICTIMS ALIVE?

There are lots of parasitic wasps. These wasps paralyze their victim then lay their eggs inside its body. When the eggs hatch, the larvae feed on the victim from inside it, while it is still alive.

ARE BEES VEGETARIAN?

Yes, bees, unlike their relatives the wasps, are vegetarian. They feed on nectar from flowers. Honeybees have tongues that are made for sucking nectar from shallow flowers. Many bumblebees have longer tongues that can push deep into tube-shaped flowers. Bees also collect pollen from flowers to take back to the nest to fed their young.

HOW MANY BEES LIVE IN A HIVE?

In a busy hive there can be up to 80,000 honeybee workers. There will be just one adult queen bee. She may live for as long as five years, and she is the most important member of the hive. The worker bees have an adult life of only about six weeks. The hive may also contain up to 200 male bees (drones) whose only job is to fertilize the queen on a mating flight. Bumblebees have much smaller nests than honeybees. The nest only lasts one season.

HOW DO BEES BECOME QUEENS?

The job that a bee does in the hive depends on what it eats. A queen bee has a special diet. The workers build some large cells for the young queens and start special treatment for them. They are fed on rich food, called royal jelly, produced by glands in the workers' heads. This allows them to develop into full queens.

WHERE IS A BEE'S SHOPPING BASKET?

Many bees have a special brush of hairs on each back leg that they use as a shopping basket. When they have collected pollen on their body hairs, they clean it off and gather it all into the pollen basket on the leg. You can often spot a well-filled, yellow pollen basket on a bee.

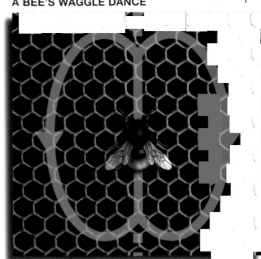

A BEE'S WAGGLE DANCE

WHY ARE BEES GOOD DANCERS?

When a bee returns from a successful trip to find pollen, it "dances" on the top of the honeycomb, surrounded by other workers. Its movements during the dance tell the other bees how far away the food source is, and the angle to the sun at which they must fly to reach it.

HOW MANY FLOWERS A DAY DOES A BEE VISIT?

A honeybee makes about 10 trips from the hive each day looking for food. It can take up to 1,000 flowers to provide enough nectar for a bee on a trip. So, it could be visiting around 10,000 flowers a day.

This bee is filling up the "basket" on its back leg with pollen.

WHY ARE BEES HAIRY?

Some bumblebees are quite good at keeping themselves warm when the outside temperature is low, and their furry bodies probably help with this. For most bees, though, a hairy body is useful mainly because it gathers up pollen grains from the flowers as it looks for nectar.

BEE COLLECTING POLLEN

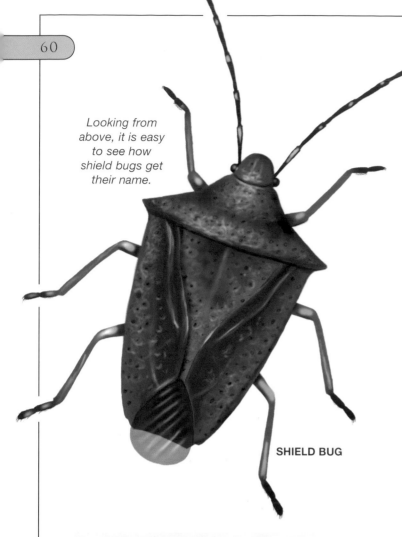

Looking from above, it is easy to see how shield bugs get their name.

SHIELD BUG

WHICH BUGS STINK?

The shield bug has quite a flat body, that looks like a shield when seen from above. They live on plants, which they eat with their piercing mouthparts. They have glands in their body which produce a smell. In some cases this smells really strong to humans, which is how this bug earned the name stink bug.

WHICH BUG FOLLOWED US FROM OUR ANCESTORS CAVES?

The bed-bug is a wingless insect that comes out at night and feeds on human blood. In the day, it hides in small, dark places. Bed-bugs attack other warm-blooded animals too. They probably first started attacking humans when our ancestors lived in caves close to other animals. Piles of skins and fur would have provided ideal hideaways. Bed-bugs are rarely a problem in hygienic modern houses.

HOW DO APHIDS CAUSE HAVOC?

Sometimes aphids damage crops just because there are so many of them sucking sap and weakening or killing the plants. In other cases the plants develop deformed leaves that make them useless to sell. Those aphids that fly from plant to plant can also spread serious diseases, injecting them into the plant as they suck sap.

WHICH BUG IS AN ASSASSIN?

Assassin bugs are predators (creatures that prey on other creatures) that use their piercing, sucking mouthparts to impale insects so that they can feed on their body fluids. They inject digestive juices and suck up the resulting "soup." They may carry their prey on their beaks. A few species suck the blood of animals.

WHAT INSECT MAKES SWEETS?

Some kinds of scaled insects produce a syrupy secretion. As the insect produces the secretion, it dries quickly in the hot climate to form sugary, honeydew lumps. It can then be eaten by humans.

HAWTHORN BUG

The hawthorn bug is a common species that feeds on hawthorn berries.

WHICH BUG SPENDS YEARS UNDERGROUND?

The periodical cicada of America has a life span of 17 years. Almost all of this time is spent as a larva underground. It digs its way through with its big front legs, and feeds on the sap of plant roots. Other cicadas also spend a lot of time underground, but the periodical cicada holds the record. After this long start, adults sometimes live for just a few weeks.

CICADA

Cicadas are among the strongest singers in the animal kingdom.

WHICH INSECT CAN COLOR FOOD?

Before the days of artificial food colorings, the red color added to food was cochineal. This is made from the crushed, dried bodies of the female cochineal bug, a kind of scale insect that feeds on cacti in Mexico.

HOW DO APHIDS DRINK PLANT JUICE?

Aphids, such as the greenfly that you find on roses, have special piercing tools on their mouths that point downward. These are pushed down into the plant vein and act just like a straw. They inject saliva down one channel of the mouthparts and suck up juices through another.

WHICH BUGS FEED ON HUMAN BLOOD?

A number of assassin bugs can feed on human blood, but most are not dangerous. One, however, is dangerous, not because of the blood it takes, but because it carries a disease. The South American bug *Triatoma infestans* carries the germ that causes Chagas' disease. This illness gives a high fever and a swollen liver, spleen, and lymph nodes.

HOW DO CICADAS SING?

Anyone who has been in a warm country has heard the loud calls of cicadas. These bugs make their sound using a kind of drumskin on each side of their abdomen. This skin is pulled in by a muscle, then allowed to snap out again, producing one click in the group of clicks that make up the cicada's song. Air sacs help to increase the sound.

HOVERFLY

Adult hoverflies feed on pollen and nectar, but their larvae eat aphids.

WHY DO SOME FLIES LOOK LIKE BEES?

By trying to look like animals with a dangerous sting, flies may stop many animals from attacking them. The hoverflies, in particular, look like and behave like bees and wasps. The hoverfly *Volucella bombylans* actually has different forms mimicking different bumblebees. It lays eggs in bumblebee nests too, where its larvae steal the food meant for the bumblebee larvae.

CAN YOU TELL A FLY BY ITS WINGS?

True flies can always be recognized among the insects because they have a single pair of wings rather than four. In fact, the rear wings have been turned into stabilizers. They are club-shaped projections (areas that stick out) from the body that give the fly information about how it is flying.

HOW DO FLIES FEED?

The fly lands on the food—a piece of meat or cheese—and spits on it to soften it. All flies have sucking mouthparts, with pumping muscles in the head, and they use these to suck up the softened food. In many flies, the tip of the mouthparts spreads out to form a sponge to absorb the liquid food. Some, such as horse-flies and mosquitoes, have piercing mouthparts, and take blood from whatever they are feeding on.

WHY DO FLIES LIKE ANIMAL DUNG?

Many species of fly lay their eggs on dung, which provides a nourishing food for the larvae. The true dung flies have legless larvae which wriggle their way about, sucking in food greedily, until they have grown enough to turn into pupae in the soil below a cow pat.

WHY ARE MOSQUITOES OUR DEADLY ENEMIES?

The female mosquito is a bloodsucker, but the diseases she may carry in her saliva are the real danger to humans. In the warmer parts of the world, there is always a danger that a mosquito is carrying the germ that causes malaria. This disease affects a large section of the world population and it makes people very weak and ill.

WHICH FLIES HELP THE POLICE WITH THEIR ENQUIRIES?

Different species of flies arrive at different stages during the rotting of flesh to lay their eggs. The larvae grow, pupate, and then turn into adults to a fast timetable. This allows a forensic scientist (scientists who study how people have died) to make a good estimate of the time of death. They look at what flies, at what stage of growth, are in a dead body.

HOW DO BLUEBOTTLES SPREAD DISEASE?

Bluebottles eat the kind of food that is likely to have bacteria on it, such as rotting vegetation or feces. Often, they will then land on our food, carrying the disease with them to infect an unfortunate human with diarrhea or worse.

The tsetse fly carries the parasite that causes sleeping sickness.

WHAT ARE "NO-SEE-UMS?"

No-see-ums are North American biting midges. They feed on us, using piercing mouthparts to take blood. Biting midges are all very small flies, but those that attack humans have an irritating bite. Being so small, they often manage to bite before being noticed, which is where the name comes from.

CAN FLIES EAT YOUR LIVING FLESH?

Some flies lay their eggs in the skin of living animals. The larvae hatch and burrow into flesh and feed on it. The warble flies eat the flesh of cattle and deer, causing much irritation. The tumbu fly larva of Africa lives under the skin of humans.

WHY DO HUMANS AVOID THE TSETSE FLY?

The tsetse fly is the insect that carries sleeping sickness and can give it to humans. The disease is quite common in wild grazing animals, and doesn't affect them badly, but it can be devastating to humans. Because it is such a serious disease, humans try to live in areas where the tsetse fly is not known to live.

TSETSE FLY

WHY DO BUTTERFLIES AND MOTHS HAVE EYESPOTS?

The eyespots on the wings of a moth or butterfly can fool a predator into thinking it is a larger animal, and therefore leaving it alone. If it is attacked, the eyespots are more noticeable than the body and head. This can be a lifesaver if a bird goes for these first, leaving the butterfly in one piece, apart from a slice out of the wing.

EMPEROR MOTH

The eyespots of the emperor moth make it look like the face of a bigger animal.

WHICH MOTH SMELLS LIKE A GOAT?

The goat moth has a larva that produces a strong smell of goat. The larva lives inside a tree for three or four years before it is mature. It can be up to 3 inches long. It can cause serious damage to the tree because it bores through the wood.

ARE MOTHS POISONOUS?

Moths do not have a poisonous bite, but many are poisonous to animals that bite them. Often their colors advertise that they have chemical defenses. The cinnabar moth has a caterpillar with black and yellow warning colors that feeds on ragwort, a plant with poisonous sap. The caterpillar isn't affected by the poison and stores it in its own body. For the rest of its life it carries the poison which only affects those that attack it, never the moth itself.

HOW DO TIGER MOTHS BAFFLE BATS?

Bats hunt tiger moths at night. The bats give out high-pitched sounds and find their prey from the echo that the sounds produce. Tiger moths have "eardrums" on their body. They hear the bats' cries and keep out of the way. They can even produce high-pitched sounds themselves to confuse the bats.

WHAT IS A SILKWORM?

The silkworm is the caterpillar of the mulberry silk moth *Bombyx mori.* Like many other moth larvae, it can make silk threads, but its cocoon is made of incredibly long threads up to $3/4$ mile long, ideal for spinning into cloth. Silkworms have been bred in captivity for at least 2,000 years in China.

WHICH BUTTERFLY IS AS BIG AS A BIRD?

The Queen Alexandra's birdwing is the biggest butterfly in the rainforest and in the world. It lives in Papua New Guinea, flitting among the tops of the rainforest trees. Female butterflies may have a wingspan of over 11 inches—twice the width of your outstretched hand! Males are much smaller. Sadly, these beautiful creatures are now very rare because of overtrapping by collectors and the destruction of their forest home.

QUEEN ALEXANDRA'S BIRDWING

In winter, monarch butterflies roost together in vast numbers.

MONARCH BUTTERFLIES

HOW FAR CAN BUTTERFLIES FLY?

Many butterflies fly very well. Red admiral and painted lady butterflies do not normally survive the winter in Britain. Some North American monarch butterflies fly to Mexico to spend the winter in huge communal roosts. They can fly 1,180 miles in just three weeks.

The Arctic clouded yellow butterfly's blood contains a special fluid that prevents it from freezing.

HOW ARE THE COLORS OF BUTTERFLIES MADE?

The wings of butterflies and moths are covered in tiny overlapping scales (their scientific name, *Lepidoptera*, means scaled wings). Each individual scale can be filled with color, giving the insect its characteristic pattern. In some butterflies, such as the shiny tropical *Morpho* butterflies, the color is produced by the special structure of the scale as much as the color on it.

ARCTIC CLOUDED YELLOW BUTTERFLY

WHAT DO BUTTERFLIES LIKE TO EAT?

Adult butterflies do not need to grow, so their food needs are for energy rather than protein. The typical butterfly food is nectar from flowers. However, some feed on sap oozing from trees, from rotting fruit, and some, including some of the most beautiful, from dung. They will also take in salts from mud.

HOW DO YOU TELL A BUTTERFLY FROM A MOTH?

Butterflies fly by day, have club-shaped antennae, and are often brightly colored. Moths fly by night, have feathery antennae, and are duller colored.

SECTION FOUR

UNDERWATER
WORLD

WHICH IS THE WORLD'S LONGEST FISH?

Oarfish are giant, eel-shaped fish that regularly grow over 20 feet long. Individuals as large as 46 feet long have been recorded. Legends of sea serpents may have been inspired by glimpses of these amazing creatures through the water.

OARFISH

WHY DO MOST FISH HAVE SLIM, TAPERING BODIES?

Most creatures that spend their whole lives in water have a sleek, streamlined shape that helps them to swim. Fish come in many different shapes and sizes. Eels are long and slender, plaice and rays are flat. Angelfish are tall and thin, so they are hard to see from the front as they approach their prey. Other fish are rounded, but almost all have a tapering shape that allows them to slip easily through the water.

WHICH IS THE TALLEST FISH?

Ocean sunfish are tall fish that can measure over 14 feet high, including their long back and belly fins. These large fish can weigh over 2 tons.

The oarfish's ribbon-like shape helps it to glide through the water.

WHAT FISH LOOKS LIKE SEAWEED?

Pipefish are long, slim, dark green fish that look just like strands of seaweed. In shallow, weedy waters, they swim upright among the seaweed fronds, and resemble their surroundings so closely that they are almost impossible to see.

Predators find it very difficult to spot pipefish hiding among strands of seaweed.

PIPEFISH

CARPET SHARK

HOW DOES THE CARPET SHARK STAY HIDDEN?

Many sea creatures have bodies with colors, shapes, and patterns that blend in with their surroundings. This natural disguise, or camouflage, helps them to hide from enemies or sneak up on their prey. Carpet sharks live and hunt on the seabed. Their pale, blotchy colors help hide them from their prey—small fish and crabs as they lie motionless on the bottom.

WHAT CREATURES PLANT A GARDEN ON THEIR BACKS?

Spider crabs make their own disguises from materials they find in the sea around them. They clip living sponges or fronds of seaweed with their strong pincers, and plant them on their backs. When the seaweed dies, they replace it with a fresh piece!

WHY DO SOME FISH HAVE BRIGHT COLORS?

Many fish that live in tropical seas are brightly colored or marked with bold spots and patterns. This coloring helps them to hide among the brightly colored coral and dark shadows, but also helps them to stand out clearly in open water. In the breeding season, when these fish are seeking mates and want to be noticed, they swim out into the open and become very obvious.

WHAT IS SLIMY AND HIDES IN ANEMONES?

In tropical seas, clownfish hide from their enemies among the stinging tentacles of sea anemones. The tentacles do not harm the clownfish, because its body is covered with a thick layer of slimy mucus, but no predator dares to come close!

WHICH FISH MAKES EYES AT ITS ENEMIES?

The twinspot wrasse has two dark patches on its back. Hunting fish may mistake the spots for the eyes of a large and possibly dangerous creature, and swim away. If this trick fails, the wrasse has another: it dives down to the seabed and quickly buries itself in the sand.

HOW DO HERRING AND MACKEREL AVOID BEING EATEN?

Fish, such as herring and mackerel, swim in groups called shoals. Living in a large group provides safety in numbers, because it is difficult for predators to single out a likely target among a shifting, shimmering mass of fish.

WHY DOES THE HERMIT CRAB NEED A HOME?

Unlike other crabs, the hermit crab has no hard case to protect it. Instead, it shelters its soft rear end inside an empty seashell. As the crab grows bigger, its shell becomes too tight, so it moves into a larger new home.

HERMIT CRAB

WHAT CREATURE GIVES A NASTY NIP?

Crabs and their relatives, lobsters, belong to a group of shelled creatures called crustaceans. The crab's soft body parts are protected by a hard outer case that forms a snug suit of armor. The creature is also armed with powerful claws, that can give a nasty nip if an enemy comes too close.

The hermit crab makes its home inside an abandoned seashell.

WHICH CREATURE THROWS INK AT ITS ENEMIES?

Cuttlefish are relatives of squid and octopus. Like their cousins, they can produce a cloud of ink to confuse their enemies. The cuttlefish jets away under cover of this "smokescreen."

Few predators will tackle a porcupine fish once it has inflated itself into a spiny ball.

PORCUPINE FISH

WHAT MAKES A PISTOL SHRIMP GO BANG?

Pistol shrimps are named after the cracking noise they make by snapping their claws. Enemies are frightened off by these unexpected "pistol shots."

WHICH FISH BLOWS ITSELF UP INTO A PRICKLY BALL?

The porcupine fish is named for the spines, like a porcupine's, that cover its body. Usually the spines lie flat against the fish's body, but if an enemy comes too close, the fish takes in water, so that its body swells to twice its normal size. It becomes a prickly ball too large and uncomfortable for predators to swallow.

WHICH CREATURE CAN GROW FOUR NEW ARMS?

The starfish is a five-limbed sea creature. If a hungry predator bites off one of its arms, the starfish can grow a new one to replace it. In fact, it can replace up to four of its arms, provided the central body of the animal is unharmed.

BLUE WHALE

WHAT RECORD-BREAKING FISH CAME BACK TO LIFE?

Coelacanths are giant primitive fish that scientists knew from fossils, but believed had died out millions of years ago. Then in 1938, a living specimen of the "extinct" species was caught off South Africa. Now scientists in submersibles have studied coelacanths living on the seabed off the island of Madagascar. Coelacanths are giant, blue-scaled fish with muscly fins which they may use to perch on the ocean bottom.

WHAT IS THE WORLD'S LARGEST MOLLUSC?

Molluscs are a family of shelled creatures that include slugs, snails, clams, and also squid and octopus. The largest mollusc is the giant squid. These creatures commonly grow to 12 feet long, but specimens as large as 69 feet have been found washed up on beaches. Scientists know little about these mysterious deep-sea creatures, which have never been seen swimming in the ocean depths.

WHICH MARINE REPTILE IS THE BIGGEST?

The saltwater crocodile is the world's largest sea-going reptile. This fierce giant grows up to 26 feet long, and its jaws and teeth are jumbo-sized to match!

ESTUARINE CROCODILE

Saltwater or estuarine crocodiles are found on eastern sea coasts from India to Australia.

Blue whales have small eyes in proportion to their giant size, but each eye is still as large as a soccer ball.

WHAT SEA CREATURE IS AS BIG AS FOUR DINOSAURS?

WHAT IS THE BIGGEST FISH?

Fish vary more in size than any other group of animals with backbones (vertebrates). The largest fish is the whale shark, which grows up to 49 feet long and weighs 22 tons. Though giant in size, whale sharks are not fierce hunters. They feed mainly on tiny shrimp-like creatures called krill.

The blue whale is the giant of the oceans. Indeed, it is the largest animal ever to have lived on Earth—four times the size of the biggest dinosaur! An adult blue whale measures up to 100 feet long, and may weigh over 220 tons—as much as 60 elephants. Female blue whales are the biggest—the males are smaller.

KILLER WHALE

WHAT IS THE SMALLEST FISH?

The dwarf goby holds the record for the world's smallest fish. Adult dwarf gobies measure only ½ inch long—about the width of your little finger. These tiny fish are found in the Indian Ocean.

Speedy orcas grow up to 30 feet long and weigh over 6 tons.

WHICH IS THE FASTEST MARINE MAMMAL?

The orca, or killer whale, is the speed champion among sea creatures. It can race along at up to 34 mph to overtake its prey.

DUGONG

Female dugongs sometimes cuddle their babies in their front flippers while they suckle, another human-like trait.

ARE MERMAIDS REAL?

In bygone times, sailors who had spent long months at sea sometimes reported seeing mermaids—creatures with the head and body of a woman and a fish's tail. Experts now believe these stories may have been inspired by dugongs—rare sea mammals with rounded faces which hold their bodies upright in the water.

WHAT FISH CARRIES THE "SWORD OF THE SEA?"

The killer whale has a tall, thin back fin 6½ feet long, that sticks straight out of the water like a sword. Another sea creature, the swordfish, has a long snout shaped like a sword, but edged with tiny teeth. This large, powerful hunter catches its prey by swimming among a shoal of fish and slashing about wildly with its "sword." There have also been reports of swordfish piercing and sinking boats.

WHICH NYMPH ATE SAILORS?

An ancient Greek legend tells of a beautiful nymph, called Scylla, who argued with the Gods and was turned into a terrifying monster by them. This horrific creature was said to have six heads, each with three rows of teeth. It lived in a sea cave, but would venture out of the deep to prey on creatures like dolphins, sharks, and even sailors!

The giant manta ray looks scary, but is generally harmless to humans.

WHAT IS A CHIMERA?

According to Greek legend, the chimera was a terrible monster with a lion's head, a goat's body, and a dragon's tail. Strange deep-sea fish called chimeras also look as if their bodies have been assembled from the parts of other creatures. They have large heads with staring eyes like bushbabies, and buck teeth like rabbits. Their bodies end in long, thin tails like rats' tails.

WHO SURVIVED BEING EATEN BY A WHALE?

According to the Bible's Old Testament, a man called Jonah was traveling by sea when a storm blew up. Superstitious sailors cast the unlucky traveler overboard. A whale swallowed Jonah, but spat him out unharmed three days later. In reality, no one could survive in a whale's stomach for three days, because there would be no air to breathe.

WHICH WHITE WHALE ATE CAPTAIN AHAB'S LEG?

Herman Melville's classic novel, *Moby Dick,* tells the story of Captain Ahab and his hunt for the great white sperm whale that tore off his leg. In his ship, the *Pequod,* Ahab and his sailors sail all around the world in search of the whale. When they finally catch up with Moby Dick, they struggle for three days to catch him. Ahab finally harpoons the great monster just as the whale sinks the ship, and the unfortunate captain is dragged down to a watery grave.

WHAT IS A MERMAID'S PURSE?

Dogfish are small sharks. The tough case in which a baby dogfish develops is called a mermaid's purse. Sometimes the empty cases are found washed up on beaches, but it is unlikely that mermaids keep their treasures there!

MANTA RAY

WHICH FISH HAS DEVIL'S HORNS?

The manta ray or devilfish has two fins that curve forward from its head like devil's horns. The ray uses its "horns" to scoop food into its mouth as it swims along the seabed.

WHAT IS A KRAKEN?

In olden days, myths and legends about dangerous sea creatures reflected the perils of ocean travel. Norwegian legends told of the kraken, a giant, many-armed monster that rose from the depths, wrapped its tentacles around unlucky ships and dragged them down to the bottom. This legend is thought to be based on sightings of the mysterious deep-sea squid.

DO UNICORNS LIVE IN THE SEA?

Narwhals are small whales that swim in icy Arctic waters. Male narwhals have a strange left tooth that grows outwards from the gum to form a long, spiraling tusk. In times past, narwhals' tusks found on beaches were sold as precious unicorn horns.

WHICH FISH CAN ATTACK WITH A SCALPEL?

Surgeonfish of tropical seas have sharp little blades like scalpels at the base of their tails. Usually the bony blades lie flat against the fish's body, but they can be flicked out like knives if an enemy approaches.

The surgeonfish defends itself by lashing its tail, which is armed with razor-sharp blades.

WHAT IS CORAL MADE OF?

Coral reefs are made by tiny creatures called polyps that live in colonies in tropical seas. Polyps are shaped like little sea anemones, but have a hard, chalky cup-shaped shell to protect their bodies. When they die, the shells remain, and new polyps grow on top of them. Over time, billions of shells build up to form a coral reef.

WHAT IS A LEAFY SEADRAGON?

The leafy seadragon is a large sea horse that lives in warm Australian water. This creature is a master of disguise. Its body is covered with long, trailing flaps of skin that look like strands of seaweed. It is very difficult to spot as it swims among the weeds.

WHAT ARE DEAD MAN'S FINGERS?

Dead man's fingers is a species of soft coral that grows on rocks. Each coral colony is made up of thousands of polyps that form a fleshy mass like a rubbery hand. When a piece of this coral washes up on the seashore, it may give swimmers a fright!

Ragged flaps of skin disguise the leafy seadragon as it drifts among the seaweed.

The Great Barrier Reef off the north-east coast of Australia is the world's largest coral reef. Stretching for 1,200 miles, it is the largest structure made by living creatures. The reef is home to many spectacular animals, including 1,500 different kinds of fish.

SURGEONFISH

SEA HORSE

WHICH FISH HAS THE HEAD OF A HORSE AND THE TAIL OF A MONKEY?

The sea horse is an unusual fish with a head shaped like the knight in a chess set. It holds its body upright and swims along by waving its back fins. It uses its long, curling tail to anchor itself in the seaweed while it searches for small creatures to eat. Its eyes can swivel independently, so the sea horse can hunt for food and watch out for enemies at the same time!

Sea horses are so bad at adapting to changes in their environment that they are now in danger of extinction.

The tripod fish uses its stiff spines like stilts to walk along the seabed.

WHICH FISH "WALKS" ON THREE LEGS?

The tripod fish is a strange fish that lives in deep, dark waters. Its two chest fins and tail fin have long, stiff spines. Together, the three spines form a tripod which the fish uses to rest and move along the seabed.

HOW DO DEEP-SEA CREATURES LIGHT UP THE DARK?

As many as 1,000 different fish make light in the deep oceans. Some have luminous bacteria living under their skin. Others have special light-producing organs, or can cause a chemical reaction that gives off light.

WHY ARE DEEP-SEA FISH MYSTERIOUS?

Scientists still know very little about deep-sea fish, because of the difficulties of descending to the ocean bottom to study them. Most deep-sea fish don't survive if they are brought to the surface. Some even explode, because their bodies are built to withstand the great pressure of the ocean depths!

HOW DO DEEP-SEA CREATURES FIND THEIR FOOD IN THE DARK?

In the black depths, many deep-sea fish sense their prey by smell, taste, and touch. A line of nerves running down the fish's body picks up vibrations in the water caused by other swimming creatures. Some deep-sea hunters have long touch- and taste-sensitive tentacles trailing from their jaws.

The hatchetfish has a line of tiny lights running down its belly that hides its shadow in the water.

HATCHETFISH

HOW DO FISH HIDE IN DARK SEAS?

Deep-sea fish are camouflaged to blend in with their surroundings. Many have black or dark bodies to match the inky waters. Others are transparent. Hatchetfish have silvery bodies that reflect any small gleams of light.

With its giant mouth, the viperfish is a fierce deep-ocean predator. The long teeth point backward to make sure no prey escapes from its jaws.

WHAT CREATURES CAN SURVIVE AT GREAT OCEAN DEPTHS?

A century ago, scientists believed that no life could exist in the very deep oceans. Now we know that creatures do survive there, but conditions are very harsh. At a depth of 3,330 feet below the sunlit surface, the water is pitch-black and very cold. Deep-sea fish must be able to stand the great pressure caused by the weight of water on top of them, which would kill surface creatures. Many deep-sea fish look like monsters from a horror film, with large heads, huge mouths with fierce teeth, and long, thin bodies. Yet most of these deep-sea horrors are very small—less than 1 foot long.

VIPERFISH

The blue-ringed octopus' spots appear if it is frightened or angry.

BLUE-RINGED OCTOPUS

WHICH IS THE WORLD'S MOST POISONOUS REPTILE?

The bite of the yellow-bellied sea snake is 50 times more powerful than that of the dreaded king cobra. Its bold yellow-and-black colors warn of danger.

WHAT BRINGS AN OCTOPUS OUT IN SPOTS?

The bite of the blue-ringed octopus is deadly poisonous. Normally, the creature's skin is sandy-colored, which helps it blend in with the seabed. But when the octopus is alarmed, bold blue rings appear all over its body. The spots act as a warning, so enemies know to keep clear.

WHAT "STONE" CAN KILL YOU IF YOU TREAD ON IT?

Over 50 different kinds of poisonous fish lurk in the world's oceans. Some are armed with venomous spines, others have poisonous flesh. The stonefish of Australian waters is one of the deadliest of all sea creatures. If a person treads on the fish, its spines release a toxin (poison) that causes agonizing pain. Numbness spreads through the victim's body, and they may die of shock, heart failure, or breathing problems.

WHAT SEA CREATURE CAN STING A PERSON TO DEATH IN FOUR MINUTES?

Jellyfish look fragile, but many species are armed with painful stings. The box jellyfish of South-east Asia is so venomous that its sting can kill a person in just four minutes. The small sea wasp jellyfish of Australia is said to have the world's most painful sting.

WHAT IS THE STINGRAY'S SECRET WEAPON?

Stingrays live and hunt on the ocean bottom. Their long, thin tails are armed with barbs that can inject a painful poison.

HOW DOES A JELLYFISH STING?

The long, trailing tentacles of jellyfish are armed with thousands of tiny stinging cells. Some cells contain tightly-coiled barbs. When a careless fish brushes against a tentacle, the barbs fire to pierce the victim's skin and release a paralyzing poison.

SEA WASP

In Australian waters, the scary sea wasp jellyfish is responsible for more deaths than sharks.

The lionfish's striped colors warn enemies to keep well away.

LIONFISH

WHY ARE LIONFISH BRIGHTLY STRIPED?

The lionfish is a beautiful but deadly fish of tropical waters. Its long, graceful spines contain a lethal poison. The lionfish drifts lazily though the water with its orange-striped coloring, yet few enemies dare to approach it. The fish's bright colors warn that it is poisonous. They are a signal known and recognized throughout the animal world.

WHAT WOULD SINK IF IT DIDN'T SWIM?

Most fish have a special organ called a swim bladder that helps them to float. Sharks have no swim bladder, so they must keep swimming to avoid sinking. Moving forward also keeps a supply of oxygen-rich sea water flowing over the shark's gills, which helps it breathe.

HAMMERHEAD SHARK

ARE ALL SHARKS DEADLY?

No. Scientists have identified about 380 different kinds of shark. Relatively few species are fierce predators that hunt large prey such as seals, squid, and penguins. Most sharks, such as whale sharks and basking sharks, feed on tiny creatures which they filter from the water using their sieve-like mouths. No harm will come to you if you meet one—unless you die of fright!

The flattened shape of the hammerhead's "hammer" may also help it float and maneuver.

WHICH SHARK HAS A HEAD LIKE A HAMMER?

The hammerhead shark is named for its curious head, shaped like a giant letter "T." The shark's eyes and nostrils are set on the ends of its "hammer." As it moves along the seabed, it swings its head from side to side. Some scientists believe that the widely spaced eyes and nostrils help the hammerhead to home in on its prey.

HOW DO SHARKS TRACK DOWN THEIR PREY?

Sharks have many senses that help with hunting. An excellent sense of smell allows the shark to detect tiny amounts of blood dissolved in the water, and track down distant wounded animals. A special sense called "distant touch" helps it to pick up vibrations caused by swimming creatures. At closer range, sensory pores on the shark's snout detect tiny electrical signals given off by prey animals' muscles. Sight and hearing also help the shark as it moves in for the kill.

WHAT MAKES ONE SHARK BITE ANOTHER?

The smell of blood sometimes excites sharks so much they go into a "feeding frenzy." A group of feeding sharks will start to snap wildly and bite one another, and may even tear one of their number to pieces in the excitement.

WHAT IS THE WORLD'S MOST DEADLY SHARK?

The great white shark is the world's most feared sea creature. It is responsible for more attacks on humans than any other shark. Great whites grow to 23 feet long. Their jaws are so powerful they can sever a human arm or leg in a single bite. Tiger and mako sharks are also known as killers.

The great white shark is nicknamed "white death." Its scientific name means "jagged teeth".

GREAT WHITE SHARK

WHAT CREATURE HOLDS THE RECORD FOR LONG-DISTANCE OCEAN TRAVEL?

Gray whales are the champion travelers of the oceans. Each year, they journey from their breeding grounds in the tropics to feeding grounds in the Arctic, and back again—a round trip of up to 12,500 miles.

GRAY WHALE

WHAT EATS ITS LUNCH IN A BUBBLE?

Humpback whales feed on small fish and krill floating near the sea surface. Sometimes they use a technique called bubble-netting to catch their prey. The whale lurks below a shoal of fish, then swims slowly upward, blowing a stream of bubbles. The fish are trapped inside the net of bubbles and cannot escape from the whale's open jaws.

Each dolphin has its own special whistle which helps the other members of its school to pinpoint its position during a hunt.

WHAT SLEEPS IN A DUVET OF SEAWEED?

The sea otter makes its home among the kelp weed beds of the eastern Pacific. While resting, the otter wraps seaweed fronds around its body so it does not drift away with the ocean currents.

CAN DOLPHINS TALK?

Dolphins make all sorts of noises, from clicks and squeals to groans and whistles. A school of hunting dolphins keep in constant touch with one another through these noises, and "talk" together to coordinate their hunt.

DOLPHINS

WHICH IS THE FRIENDLIEST SEA CREATURE?

Dolphins are naturally playful and friendly to humans. They often swim alongside boats, riding on the bow-wave. Dolphins called "friendlies" regularly visit tourist beaches to swim with holiday-makers. There are many reports of dolphins rescuing drowning people, and even saving swimmers from sharks.

WHAT HUNTS BY SONAR?

Dolphins hunt with the aid of their own built-in sonar system, called echolocation. As they swim along, they produce a stream of clicking sounds. Sound waves from the clicks spread out through the water. When they hit an object, such as a shoal of fish, they bounce back. The dolphin can sense the size and movements of its prey by listening to the echoes.

Gray whales swim such huge distances on migration that scientists use satellites to track them.

WHICH IS THE CLEVEREST SEA CREATURE?

Dolphins are among the world's most intelligent creatures. Tests in aquariums show they learn to perform new tasks quickly, and can even pass on their skills by "talking" to dolphins in other tanks. Sea otters are clever too, for they are one of the few animals able to use tools. The otter feeds on sea urchins, crabs, and other shelled creatures. It breaks open the shells by smashing them against a flat rock balanced on its chest.

SEA OTTER

The sea otter is a skillful tool-user

WHY DO WHALES AND DOLPHINS COME TO THE SURFACE?

Whales and dolphins look a lot like fish, but they are really sea-going mammals. Like all mammals, they breathe oxygen from the air, and so must surface to breathe. One or two nostrils called blowholes on top of the animal's head allow it to breathe without lifting its head from the water. But dolphins and some whales sometimes rear right out of the water to look around, a technique called spy-hopping.

LIFE IN ARID LANDS

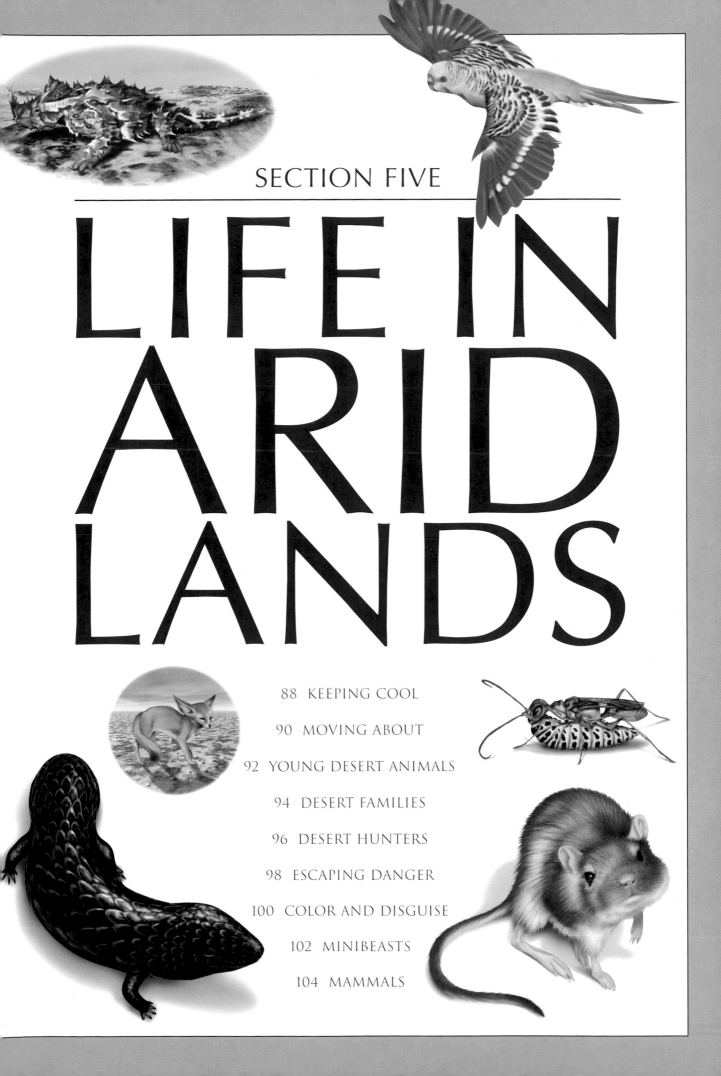

HOW DO DESERT ANIMALS KEEP COOL?

Deserts are hot, dry places where almost no rain falls. Each day, the sun beats down fiercely from cloudless skies. At first glance, deserts seem lifeless places, but in fact all kinds of creatures live there. Many desert animals spend the scorching midday hours in underground burrows. Burrow-dwellers include snakes, lizards, and tortoises, rodents and other mammals, and even some kinds of birds.

DO MANY DESERT ANIMALS HAVE LARGE EARS?

Fennec foxes of the Sahara Desert have large pointed ears. So do kit foxes of American deserts, and also desert hedgehogs. All these creatures' ears work in the same way as the jack rabbit's do. They radiate heat to keep the animal cool.

WHY IS DEW THE DEVIL'S FAVORITE DRINK?

The thorny devil is a lizard of American deserts. Its body is covered with sharp spines that protect it from enemies. The spines also act as a water-catchment system. On cold nights dew condenses on the animal's body. Moisture runs down grooves in the spines straight into the lizard's mouth.

Fennec foxes are the world's smallest foxes, but have the largest ears of any fox.

FENNEC FOX

HOW DO COLD-BLOODED CREATURES COPE WITH THE HEAT?

Snakes, lizards, and many other reptiles live in deserts. Reptiles are cold-blooded creatures—their body temperature is not controlled by a thermostat in their body like ours is, but by their surroundings. Throughout the day, they change their position to regulate their temperature so they can stay active. A desert lizard basks in the sun in the early morning to warm up. When the sun blazes down at midday, it moves into the shade to cool off. It sunbathes again in the evening so its body stays warm at night.

The thorny devil drinks dew channeled by its spines.

WHICH DESERT CREATURE HAS A BUILT-IN SUNSHADE?

Ground squirrels of American and South African deserts have long, bushy tails. When searching for food in the hot sun, the squirrel fluffs out its tail and holds it over its head to act as a shady parasol.

GROUND SQUIRREL

DO DESERT CREATURES EVER SLEEP FOR LONG PERIODS?

Some desert creatures, such as tortoises, enter a deep sleep called aestivation to avoid the hottest summer weather. In harsh Mongolian deserts, furry mammals called susliks sleep out the scorching summer and hibernate in winter too. Aestivation comes from the Latin word for summer, and hibernation from the Latin word for winter.

Ground squirrels use their tails to shade themselves from the baking sun. In the very hottest weather they retreat to their underground burrows.

WHICH SNAKE MOVES SIDEWAYS?

Sidewinder snakes of North America are so-called because they move by looping their body and slithering sideways. Scales on the underside of the snake's body grip the sand. As it passes, the sidewinder leaves a line of parallel tracks across the desert.

As it slithers sideways, only a small part of the sidewinder's body touches the burning sand.

KANGAROO RAT

SIDEWINDER

WHICH HUGE DESERT BIRDS ARE CHAMPION RUNNERS?

Ostriches live in deserts and dry grasslands in Africa. These large, heavy birds can't fly, but they have very powerful legs and can race along at speeds of up to 45 mph. They are the fastest creatures on two legs!

WHICH DESERT ANIMAL HAS WEBBED FEET?

Most animals with webbed feet live near water. The web-footed gecko lives in the Namib Desert in southern Africa. Its webbed feet help it to run on fine sand without sinking in.

WHICH LIZARD MOVES LIKE A FISH?

Sandfish are African lizards with long, slender bodies like eels. They move through the sand by thrashing their body from side to side like a fish swimming in water. The sandfish's feet have scaly fringes that can help it run along the sand.

WHICH LIZARD DANCES TO COOL OFF?

Most lizards use all four legs for running. The bearded lizard of Australian deserts is different—it runs on its hind legs to keep its body off the sand. When standing still, it cools its feet by "dancing"— lifting each of its legs in turn.

WHEN IS A KANGAROO REALLY A RAT?

Kangaroo rats have strong, springy hind legs shaped like a kangaroo's legs. As they bound along at high speed, their paws make little contact with the burning ground. These rodents also leap high in the air to reach the young, tasty shoots of desert shrubs. Jerboas of African and Asian deserts are rodents with very similar hind legs that live in the same way.

WHICH GOLDEN MAMMAL "SWIMS" THROUGH SAND?

The golden mole lives in South Africa. Its forelegs have large, flat claws that help it to shovel sand aside as it burrows under the surface. Its digging action is like a swimmer's breaststroke. This little beast can dig a tunnel 2½ miles long in a single night.

GOLDEN MOLE

Kangaroo rats live in North American deserts.

Golden moles leave tell-tale ridges of sand on the surface as they burrow underground.

WHAT WEARS SNOW-SHOES WITH HAIRY SOLES?

Desert animals such as camels and addax antelopes have very broad feet. Their feet act like snowshoes, spreading the animal's weight over a wide area to stop it sinking into soft sand. Hot sand can scorch tender animal feet, so the camel's feet have tough soles to protect them. Some other desert beasts such as sand cats and gerbils have feet with hairy soles for the same reason.

WHAT LARGE BIRDS MAKE CARING FATHERS?

Female emus lay their eggs in the male birds'
nests, and the father sits on the
eggs to incubate them.
When the chicks hatch
out they follow
their father for
18 months.

*An emu chick sheltering
from the sun beneath its
father's large body.*

EMUS

WHICH ANIMALS EMPLOY A NANNY?

Young meerkats are born in the safety of the underground colony. Like all mammals, they feed on their mother's milk. Female meerkats known as "nannies" look after the babies when their mothers go off to feed.

WHAT DO BUDGIES FEED THEIR YOUNG?

Budgies feed their chicks on a pale fluid known as "budgie milk." The females make this nutritious liquid in their throats and feed it to their babies with their beaks. After about a month, the young budgies are strong enough to fly and leave the nest.

HOW DO SCORPIONS LOOK AFTER THEIR YOUNG?

Most minibeasts take little care of their young, but female scorpions are protective mothers. The young ride round on their mother's back, safe beneath her sting. After three weeks they are strong enough to drop off and fend for themselves.

WHICH CHICK DRINKS FROM ITS FATHER'S FEATHERS?

Sandgrouse are birds of South African deserts. They fly a long way to drink water daily. The male bird also visits the waterhole to bring water to his thirsty chicks. He wades in and soaks up water with his fluffy breast feathers. When he flies back to the nest, the chicks drink from his soggy feathers.

WHAT HAPPENS TO ANT LIONS WHEN THEY GROW UP?

Ant lions are young, wingless insects with fat bodies. The adult insects are long, delicate winged creatures like dragonflies. When the ant lion is fully grown it changes into a pupa (chrysalis). As it rests inside the hard pupa case, its body is transformed. Eventually the case splits open and a beautiful winged insect climbs out.

WHICH CREATURE HATCHES IN TWO DAYS AND GROWS UP IN TWO WEEKS?

Spadefoot toads spend most of the year buried in the mud. When rain falls, they emerge and breed quickly before the pool dries up again. The females lay their eggs in the water, and the tadpoles hatch after only two days. Most tadpoles take months to grow up, but spadefoot tadpoles become adults in just two weeks. As the pool dries out and turns to mud, the young toads bury themselves to wait for the next shower of rain.

Marsupial moles spend most of their lives underground and have very poor vision.

MARSUPIAL MOLE

WHICH DESERT BEAST REARS ITS YOUNG IN A POUCH?

Marsupials are a group of mammals that rear their young in a pouch. Marsupial moles live underground in Australian deserts. The mother's pouch opens backward, toward the tail, so sand does not smother the baby as she burrows along.

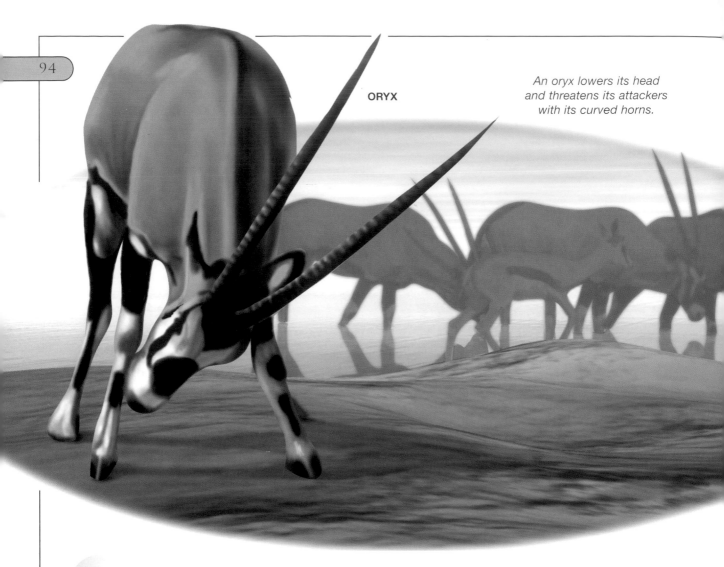

ORYX

An oryx lowers its head and threatens its attackers with its curved horns.

WHY IS THERE SAFETY IN NUMBERS?

Oryx are large antelope that live in herds in African and Arabian deserts. The herd provides safety in numbers because a hunter, such as a big cat, will find it difficult to target a single victim in a great herd. The oryx usually canter off to escape from danger, but if these beasts are cornered, they defend themselves with their horns.

WHICH CREATURE GIVES INSTRUCTIONS IN SCENT?

Naked mole rats are strange, blind mammals that live in underground burrows in Africa. The colony is ruled by a female, called the queen, who alone gives birth to young. She communicates with the other mole rats by giving off special scent signals, known as pheromones, which tell the group what to do.

WHAT BIRDS RUN AFTER CLOUDS?

Emus live in flocks in dry parts of Australia. These giant birds feed on plants, fruit, insects, and lizards. They cannot fly, but roam the land on foot looking for food. Farmers build long stretches of tall fences to prevent emus from destroying their crops. In times of drought, emus watch for rain clouds and run after them in search of places where rain has fallen.

WHICH INSECTS DO DESERT PEOPLE FEAR THE MOST?

Locusts are large grasshoppers found in African and Asian deserts. When their plant food is plentiful, they breed quickly and gather in huge groups called swarms. A locust swarm may contain many millions of insects; as it flies off in search of food, it turns the sky black. Farmers fear these insects because a giant swarm can destroy many acres of carefully tended crops in minutes, causing whole villages to go hungry.

BUDGERIGAR

The budgerigar is a member of the parakeet family.

WHICH DESERT BIRDS ARE NOMADS?

Budgerigars live in flocks in the Australian outback. They have no fixed home, but fly on continually in search of areas where rain has fallen and plants are producing seeds, their favorite food. When seeds are plentiful, the budgies take their chance to settle temporarily, make nests, and rear their young.

Meerkat guards bark to warn the rest of the colony if an enemy approaches.

WHY DOES A MEERKAT STAND ON ITS HIND LEGS?

Many different desert animals live in groups. Meerkats are furry mammals that live in a network of underground tunnels called a colony. These animals cooperate so they can feed safely above ground. One meerkat stands up on its hind legs and keeps a sharp eye out for enemies, such as snakes and hawks, while the rest feed. If the sentry spots a predator, it gives a warning bark and the group quickly disappears.

MEERKAT GROUP

WHAT DESERT BIRDS ARE ARMED AND DANGEROUS?

Lanner falcons of the Sahara Desert are fierce birds of prey. They have strong feet with razor-sharp claws called talons, and a deadly hooked beak to tear prey animals apart.

LANNER FALCON

Falcons usually have pointed wings and a notch in the top of their beaks.

WHAT SQUEEZES ITS PREY TO DEATH?

King snakes of the American deserts do not have a poisonous bite. Instead, they kill their prey by constriction. The snake wraps its body around a victim such as a rat, and squeezes tighter and tighter. The victim cannot breathe and soon dies of suffocation.

Caracals leap as high as 6.5 feet in the air to capture flying birds.

WHICH CAT CAN SNATCH AN EAGLE FROM THE AIR?

The caracal hunts birds, antelope, mice, and lizards. It can put on a burst of speed to overtake a racing antelope, and can also leap high in the air to catch desert birds. This fierce cat can kill even a large bird like an eagle with one swipe of its powerful paw.

CARACAL

WHY ARE WATERHOLES DANGEROUS?

Hungry lanner falcons hunt by lurking at waterholes. When birds, such as sandgrouse, fly in to drink at the pool, the falcon pounces and seizes a victim in its talons.

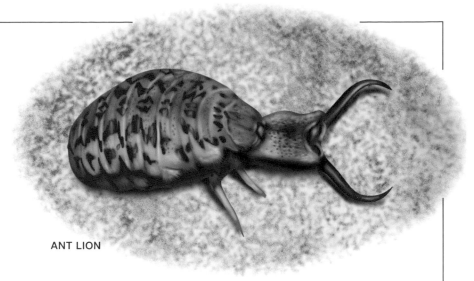

ANT LION

WHICH DOG STEALS A BIG CAT'S DINNER?

Jackals live in the deserts and grasslands of Africa. They hunt in packs and scavenge whatever food they can find. Small mammals, reptiles, birds, and fruit are all on the jackal's menu. They also steal meat from kills made by other hunters, such as lions, using clever teamwork to fool the lion. One jackal distracts the hunter while another sneaks up and pulls the meat away.

WHY DOES THE ANT LION BURY ITSELF IN A PIT?

Strange creatures called ant lions are the young of desert insects that look like dragonflies. The ant lion is a cunning hunter. It digs a small funnel-shaped pit in the sand, then buries itself in the bottom and lies in wait. When a victim, such as an ant, falls into the pit, the ant lion pounces, and grabs its prey in its powerful jaws.

HOW DOES THE RATTLESNAKE KILL ITS PREY?

A striking rattlesnake sinks its poison fangs into its victim. Then it lets the animal go. The rat runs off, but is soon overcome by the snake's venom and drops to the ground. The rattlesnake catches up and swallows its victim whole.

WHAT IS THE FASTEST ANIMAL IN THE WORLD?

Cheetahs live in dry grasslands in Africa. These sleek, lithe cats can race along at speeds of up to 62 mph to outrun fast prey such as gazelles.

The cheetah is the fastest animal in the world.

CHEETAH

DESERT TORTOISE

The tortoise's shell stops it from drying out.

WHAT WEARS ARMOR IN THE DESERT?

The desert tortoise moves far too slowly to outrun its enemies. Instead, it has an armor-plated shell made up of many bony plates fused together. When it is threatened, the reptile pulls its head and limbs inside the shell so a hunter cannot reach the soft parts of its body.

WHAT LOSES ITS TAIL TO SAVE ITS LIFE?

A web-footed gecko's tail helps it to balance when running, but it is not vital to the creature's survival. If a hunting bird seizes the tail, it breaks off at a special point and the gecko escapes. Its muscles contract to stop the bleeding. In time, a new tail grows on the stump.

WHEN DOES AN OWL SOUND LIKE A SNAKE?

Burrowing owls of American deserts are talented mimics. They can make a hissing, rattling noise that sounds like an angry rattlesnake. The noise frightens away most predators trying to enter the owl's burrow.

WHAT PUTS UP ITS HOOD AND SPITS POISON?

The red cobra is a poisonous snake that lurks by waterholes in East Africa. When danger threatens, the cobra raises the skin round its neck to make a threatening hood. If an intruder, such as a person, does not back away, the snake spits poison into its victim's eyes. Humans who've been attacked can go blind if their eyes are not treated quickly.

WHAT IS THE DOMINO BEETLE'S SECRET WEAPON?

The domino ground beetle has a secret weapon. It can produce a jet of burning chemicals from its abdomen (rear end), which it squirts in the face of enemies to ward off attack.

WHY MIGHT A FOX GET A MOUTHFUL OF PRICKLES?

Desert hedgehogs live in North Africa and Arabia. If a predator, such as a fennec fox, attacks, the hedgehog curls up into a ball. Tough spines protect its back, and the fox cannot reach its head and soft belly.

DESERT HEDGEHOG

WHAT JAMS ITSELF IN A CRACK?

Chuckwalla lizards live in deserts in the western United States. If danger threatens, the lizard speeds into a crack in the rock, then fills its body with air so it swells up. It jams itself into the crevice so a predator, such as a kit fox, cannot pull it out.

WHAT MAKES THE KANGAROO RAT JUMP?

Kangaroo rats leap high in the air to avoid enemies such as snakes and foxes. Their darting leaps confuse the predator, and they may also kick sand in its face before racing away.

A fox attempting to attack a desert hedgehog will end up with a mouthful of prickles.

DOMINO BEETLE

WHAT COLORS WARN THAT THE GILA MONSTER IS POISONOUS?

The poisonous gila monster lizard has orange and black stripes on its scaly skin. These colors are common to poisonous creatures all over the world, so they act as a warning sign that the creature is dangerous. Other animals recognize the colors and know to avoid the lizard.

WHY DOES THE SAND CAT SEEM INVISIBLE?

The sand cat's fur is browny-yellow in color, with dark markings on its head, legs, and tail. These subtle colors and patterns, known as camouflage, blend in with its surroundings so the cat can hunt without being seen. It stalks prey, such as jerboas, by approaching stealthily with its body flattened against the rocks, until it is close enough to pounce. The sand cat lives in African and Asian deserts.

WHICH CREATURE SEEMS TO HAVE TWO HEADS?

The Australian shingleback lizard has a short, plump tail that acts as a fat store. The tail also provides good camouflage to confuse predators. It looks very like the lizard's stumpy head, so enemies don't know which end to attack.

WHY IS THE KING SNAKE ORANGE AND BLACK?

The king snake of American deserts is not poisonous. But its orange and black stripes mimic the colors of the deadly coral snake of the same region. Enemies are fooled by its disguise and will not go near it, thinking it is a coral snake.

Predators looking at the "two heads" of the shingleback lizard don't know which end might bite back.

SHINGLEBACK LIZARD

Vibrant markings, like those on the domino beetle, show that a creature is poisonous.

WHEN DOES A SQUIRREL LOOK LIKE AN ANTELOPE?

Antelope squirrels of American deserts use camouflage to hide from their enemies. The squirrel has mainly brown fur, with a white stripe like an antelope's running down its body. The stripe helps to break up its outline, making it hard for enemies to spot. If danger threatens, the squirrel freezes and becomes almost invisible against the rocks and sand.

HOW DID THE DOMINO BEETLE GET ITS NAME?

The domino beetle is so-called because the white spots on its black body make it look like a domino. This coloration also acts as a warning signal, showing that the beetle is armed with poisonous chemicals. Predators that have been sprayed with poison once will avoid these beetles in future.

WHICH SNAKE WAITS IN THE SAND FOR ITS DINNER?

The sand viper of North African and Arabian deserts is light brown in color. The snake hunts by lying in wait for passing lizards and other small creatures. It chooses a spot where it can wriggle down into the loose sand. More sand blows over its body and soon only the head and watchful eyes can be seen. The viper's perfect disguise has an added advantage: it is also cooler under the desert sand.

WHEN IS A GERBIL RELIEVED TO LOSE ITS TAIL?

Gerbils are mainly sandy-colored, so they blend in well with the Mongolian desert. But the rodent has a tuft of dark hair on its tail. If a predator, such as a fox, spots the creature moving, it will attack the dark tail end, which is easier to see than the head. If the fox manages to grab the gerbil's tail it can break off, giving the animal a chance to escape, though its tail will not grow again.

WHICH SPIDER EATS UNTIL IT DROPS?

Camel spiders of African deserts are greedy hunters. They can eat as many as 100 insects in a day, and sometimes get so full they can hardly walk. The camel spider hunts at night, and before it has eaten it can move very quickly. Its front legs have special suckers so it can run straight up smooth walls, to grab lizards and even small birds in its powerful jaws.

WHAT INSECTS DO PEOPLE LIKE TO EAT?

Young insects called wichetty grubs are a favorite food of Australian Aborigines. These grubs live underground on tree roots. Aborigines dig them up and eat them raw or cooked. In African deserts, people also eat grasshoppers and other insects.

HOW DOES THE JEWEL WASP GET ITS NAME?

The jewel wasp of western America is named for the bright metallic colors on its body case, which make it look like a gleaming jewel.

WHY DOES A SCORPION HAVE HAIRY LEGS?

Scorpions have poor eyesight, but a keen sense of touch and smell. Their legs are covered with tiny sensitive bristles. The little hairs can detect vibrations caused by other creatures' movements. The scorpion can tell the size of its prey from the signals it receives.

HOW DO SCORPIONS EAT MICE AND LIZARDS?

Scorpions catch quite large prey, such as mice and lizards, but they only have tiny mouths. They smother their prey in digestive juices. Their powerful pincers help pull the animal apart and crush it to a crunchy mush, which the scorpion sucks into its mouth.

HOW DOES THE JEWEL WASP FEED ITS YOUNG?

When the jewel wasp is ready to lay its eggs, it digs a burrow and then goes hunting. It catches a cockroach and paralyzes it with its sting. Then it drags its victim back to the burrow and lays an egg on it. When the wasp larva hatches out, it enjoys live cockroach meat.

JEWEL WASP

A female jewel wasp drags a victim back to her nest. Her young are legless, because they do not need to move to find their food.

WHY DO HONEYPOT ANTS TAKE INSECTS PRISONER?

Honeypots ants live in a colony. Most kinds feed on nectar from flowers, but some get their food in an amazing way. They capture aphids or cochineal insects and keep them captive in their nest. The ants stroke their prisoners with their antennae (feelers), to make the insects produce honeydew, a sweet liquid, for the colony to drink.

HONEYPOT ANTS

HOW DO HONEYPOT ANTS GET THEIR NAME?

Honeypot ants that feed on flower nectar run low in food in the long dry season. But they have a clever way of storing food. When flowers are plentiful, they feed the nectar to special ants called repletes. The bodies of these ants swell up so they become living honey stores (or honeypots). The repletes feed the other ants when food is scarce.

In Australia, Aborigines eat honeypot ants like candy.

The two-humped bactrian and one-humped dromedary camel.

HOW MANY HUMPS DO CAMELS HAVE?

There are two different types of camel. Arabian camels (dromedaries) have a single hump. They are found in North Africa as well as Arabia. Bactrian camels come from the Gobi Desert and other dry parts of Asia. These hairy beasts have not one hump, but two.

WHAT IS A CAMEL'S HUMP MADE OF?

A camel's hump does not contain water, as some people think. In fact, it is a store of fat which the animal can live off when food is scarce. An Arabian camel's hump shrinks as the fat inside is used up in hard times. A bactrian camel's hump flops over.

HOW DO ECHIDNAS EAT THEIR MEALS?

The echidna or spiny anteater is an unusual mammal found in the Australian outback. It feeds on insects and termites, which it slurps up with its long, sticky tongue.

ECHIDNA

Jack rabbits of North American deserts are champion racers. They can speed along at up to 35 mph, to outdistance predators such as foxes.

Gerbils are desert rodents that feed mainly on seeds.

GERBIL

WHERE DO GERBILS STORE THEIR FOOD?

When the gerbil finds a good food source, its stuffs the pouches in its cheeks with seeds. Then it returns to the safety of its burrow to feast in peace.

WHY IS THE CAMEL CALLED THE SHIP OF THE DESERT?

Camels are strong, hardy beasts that have been domesticated (tamed) for thousands of years. Before the days of trucks and planes, they were used to ferry heavy loads across the desert, where the huge sand dunes often look like waves. Camels are also used as riding animals, but their rolling walk gives a bumpy ride, rather like a boat in a choppy sea. It makes some riders "seasick!"

WHY DON'T CAMELS GET SAND UP THEIR NOSES AND IN THEIR EYES?

Windy deserts are no problem for camels. Their nostrils close between breaths to keep the sand out, and long eyelashes protect their eyes from blowing sand. In sandstorms they shut their eyes, but can see well enough through their thin eyelids to keep moving if necessary.

WHAT MAKES ITS NEST IN A CACTUS BUSH?

Pack rats build their nests in cactus bushes in North American deserts. They pile more cacti up around the nest to deter predators, such as foxes, and leave only a tiny entrance hole so the fox cannot get in. The nest contains several cool, comfy chambers where the pack rats sleep by day.

KINGS OF THE JUNGLE

THE RAINFOREST CANOPY

Little sunlight reaches the forest floor, which is dark, gloomy, and thick with rotting leaves.

HOW DO RAINFORESTS GROW?

Rainforests grow in layers, depending on the height of the trees. At the very top is the emergent layer where the tallest trees poke out above the rest. Beneath is a thick layer of treetops called the canopy, growing like a leafy, green umbrella over the rainforest. Below that is the understorey, made up of smaller trees and saplings.

WHY ARE THEY CALLED RAINFORESTS?

Because of where they grow, rainforests are hot and wet all year round. There are no real seasons—just hot and wet, and even hotter and wetter. On the wettest days, up to 10 inches of rain can fall, and there are thunderstorms in the afternoons.

HOW MANY ANIMALS LIVE IN THE RAINFORESTS?

Although rainforests cover only about a tenth of the Earth's surface, they are home to at least half of the world's species of animals and plants—that's thousands of insects alone. About 1.5 million people also live in the rainforests.

AYE-AYE

Lemurs are closely related to monkeys and live in trees.

ARE THERE MORE ANIMALS TO BE DISCOVERED?

Yes, there are! Scientists believe that there may be many more animals, especially insects, that they have never seen or identified. Every so often, they discover a new one. Part of the problem is that many rainforest animals are nocturnal—they only come out at night. Others rarely venture down from their treetop homes.

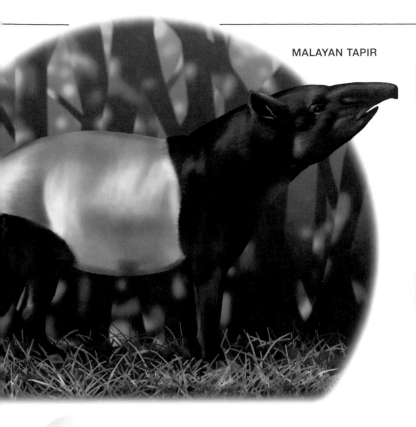

MALAYAN TAPIR

WHAT IS BEING DONE TO SAVE THEM?

All over the world, conservation groups are working hard to save the rainforests. If the destruction is not stopped, the forests will disappear in 50 years' time. We will then lose millions of animals, plants, and precious resources like rainforest plants that could be used to make medicine.

WHY ARE RAINFORESTS BEING CUT DOWN?

Rainforests were once twice the size they are today, and they are disappearing fast. To clear land for farming and cattle ranching, the forests are being cut down and burned at the rate of 60 soccer pitches worth every single minute.

Jaguars like to live close to water where they can fish for food.

WHERE DO MOST RAINFOREST ANIMALS LIVE?

Most rainforest animals, from large, sleepy sloths to tiny insects, live in the thick layer of trees that makes up the canopy. This is the layer that gets most sun and rain. Here the trees produce plenty of fruit, seeds, leaves, and flowers—a feast for the animals.

WHERE IS THE BIGGEST RAINFOREST?

The world's biggest rainforest grows in South America, along the banks of the River Amazon. It is bigger than all the other rainforests put together. At 3,862 miles, the River Amazon is the world's second longest river, next to Egypt's River Nile.

JAGUAR

WHAT BIRD IS LIKE A HELICOPTER?

Hummingbirds feed on nectar found deep inside rainforest flowers in South America. To reach its food, a hummingbird hovers in front of a flower like a tiny helicopter. It has to beat its wings up to 20 times a second, so quickly that they make a humming sound. Then the bird probes into the flower with its long, thin bill and laps up the nectar with its tube-like tongue. A hummingbird can also fly forward and backward, and up and down.

WHICH ANIMALS BOUNCE ACROSS THE GROUND?

Sifakas are lemurs from Madagascar. They can't run on all fours because their legs are much longer than their arms. Instead they bounce along the ground, hopping from one foot to the other, holding their arms up in the air.

WHY DO FROGS HAVE SUCKERS ON THEIR FEET?

Many rainforest frogs live high up in the trees to avoid hungry predators on the ground. They have to be good at climbing. To help them, they have pads of sticky hairs, like suckers, on their fingers and toes, and loose, sticky skin on their bellies for grip. If they land in a tree with plenty of lizards to eat, they may not move off it for months on end.

HOW DO GIBBONS SWING SO FAST?

Gibbons have arms that are longer than their bodies. This helps them to swing very fast through the trees. With its huge armspan, a gibbon can swing 32 feet from one branch to another in one go, gripping the branches with its long fingers. Gibbons live in the rainforests of South-east Asia.

WHICH CREATURE PERFORMS A MIRACLE?

The basilisk lizard uses its water-walking skills to escape from enemies.

The basilisk lizard of South America has an amazing ability. It walks on water! It literally runs across the surface of a pond or pool without sinking. It is thought that its sheer speed keeps it afloat, while its long tail helps it to balance.

BASILISK LIZARD

HOW DO SNAKES CLIMB TREES?

Many rainforest snakes are excellent climbers. Their long, muscular bodies are good for slithering along the branches, and they have rough scales on their bellies to help them grip. Then they loop their coils over a branch and lie in wait for prey.

CAN SNAKES FLY?

Snakes can't really fly because they don't have wings. But some have a go. The paradise flying snake lives high up in the rainforest trees in Borneo. To set off in search of lizards to eat, it launches itself from a branch and flattens its body so that it can glide through the trees. These snakes are also excellent climbers, with sharp ridges on their bellies for grip.

Spider monkeys live in Central and South America.

HOW MANY LEGS DOES A SPIDER MONKEY HAVE?

The answer is four, like any other monkey! But spider monkeys also use their long tails as an extra arm or leg for gripping on to branches. In fact, their tails are so strong that the monkeys can swing by their tails alone.

*The howler monkey
has a special voice
box that allows it to
howl loudly.*

WHICH ANIMALS USE THEIR TAILS LIKE FLAGS?

When ring-tailed lemurs go for
a walk through the forests of
Madagascar to patrol their
territory, each lemur keeps its
stripy tail raised high in the air.
This is a signal to the other
lemurs, like someone waving a
flag. It shows them where each
lemur is and helps to keep the
group together. The lemurs
mark the trees in their territory
with a smelly scent to warn
other ring-tails to keep out.

WHICH RAINFOREST ANIMAL SHOUTS LOUDEST?

Of all the animals in the rainforest, the howler
monkey has the loudest voice. It lives high up in
the forests of South America. Every morning and
evening, groups of howler monkeys wail and
roar in an ear-splitting chorus.

WHY DO TENRECS SPIT?

A tenrec is a prickly, hedgehog-like animal from Madagascar. It sets out its territory by spitting on the spot it wants to mark, then rubbing its own strong body smell on to the wet spot. Other tenrecs recognize the smell and stay away.

WHICH MONKEY TURNS RED WITH RAGE?

Many monkeys have brightly colored skin or hair to signal to others. The odd-looking uakari lives in the rainforests of South America. Its face goes red if it is angry or excited. Uakaris also go bright red in the sun.

WHICH BIRD SOUNDS LIKE A BELL?

To attract a mate, the male bellbird of Central and South America opens its mouth wide and makes a call that sounds like a large, clanging bell. The bellbird has the loudest voice of any bird, so loud it can be heard over half a mile away.

WHICH ANIMAL BURPS A LOT?

Male orangutans of South-east Asia burp loudly to warn other males to keep out of their territory. They fill the saggy pouches of skin around their throats with air, then let out a long call that starts off as a loud roar and ends with bubbling burps and groans.

WHY DO TARSIERS HAVE SUCH BIG EYES?

Tarsiers are tiny, monkey-like animals from South-east Asia. They come out to feed at night. They use their enormous eyes and sensitive ears to help them locate their prey of insects, lizards and birds in the dark. Then they leap through the branches, grab their prey in both hands and gobble it down head first.

WHICH ANIMAL USES SEMAPHORE?

It can be difficult to be heard in the noisy rainforests of South America. So many animals turn to color to attract attention. Frogs usually communicate by croaking, but if it's too noisy, they wave their brightly colored legs at each other in a type of froggy semaphore. Monkeys wail and roar in an ear-splitting chorus. They do this to defend their own special patch of forest and their own particular food trees. You can't miss their call. Their voices are so loud that they can be heard some 5 miles away.

WHY DOES THE MOUSE DEER STAMP ITS FEET?

Mouse deer live in Asia. They are about the size of hares, with short, thin legs. They stamp their tiny feet to signal to each other. Mouse deer are extremely nervous. When they are startled, they freeze, then run away in a zigzag through the forest.

MOUSE DEER

Mouse deer have two teeth that stick out from their top jaw.

WHICH BIRD IMPRISONS ITSELF IN A TREE?

In Africa, a female hornbill lays her eggs in a hole in a tree. Then, helped by her mate, she seals herself in, covering the entrance with droppings and mud. Only a tiny slit is left, through which the male delivers food. This keeps the nest safe from snakes until the chicks are old enough to leave the nest and learn how to fly.

WHAT WASP LAYS ITS EGGS IN THE BODY OF A LIVE INSECT?

In many rainforests, female ichneumon wasps lay their eggs in the body of another insect while it is still alive. When the eggs hatch, the wasp grubs feed on the insect. They leave its vital parts until last, to keep it alive and fresh for longer. Scary!

BLUE BIRD OF PARADISE

Birds of paradise live in Australia and Papua New Guinea.

WHICH BIRD HANGS UPSIDE DOWN TO SHOW OFF?

The dazzling feathers of male birds of paradise give the birds their names. People thought that these birds were so stunning they could only come from paradise. The males use their feathers to attract a mate. The Count Raggi's bird of paradise puts on a special courtship display. He hangs upside down from a branch to show off his magnificent orange feathers. After mating, he loses his feathers and has to grow them again the following year.

WHICH INSECT SINGS TO ITS MATE?

The cicada is the loudest insect in the rainforest. To attract a mate, the male cicada clicks small plates of skin in its sides at a rate of more than 1,000 times a second. Meanwhile, it listens for a female to reply with a flick of her wings. Cicadas live in rainforests all over the world.

WHICH BABY BIRD HAS CLAWS ON ITS WINGS?

This hoatzin chick makes a dive for safety as its parent looks on.

Hoatzins live in South America. They build their nests in trees that overhang rainforest rivers and streams. If danger threatens, hoatzin chicks simply dive headfirst into the river. When it is safe, the chicks climb slowly back up, using tiny claws on their wings to help them grip.

HOATZIN ADULT AND CHICK

WHY DO GLOW-WORMS GLOW?

At night, some rainforest trees are filled with tiny flashing lights. These are made by glowworms or fireflies. They produce their yellow-green lights through chemical reactions inside their bodies. Glowworms flash their lights in the dark to attract a mate. Each species has its own pattern of flashes, which other members of its species can recognize. Despite the name, glowworms are actually a type of beetle.

WHICH CATERPILLARS LIVE IN A TENT?

The tent-caterpillar moth of South America gets its name from the way its caterpillars live. They build fine, silk nests among the rainforest trees. The adult moths are superbly camouflaged to blend in with the lichens growing on a tree trunk.

115

WHAT DO ORANGUTANS USE AS UMBRELLAS?

It rains almost every day in the rainforest. Some animals don't mind the rain, but orangutans try to avoid a soaking. If they are caught in a shower, they pick a large leaf for an umbrella and shelter beneath it until the rain stops. Orangutans live in the rainforests of Borneo and Sumatra in South-east Asia.

ORANGUTAN

WHO LIVES IN A TREE ANT'S NEST?

Tree ants, of course! But when the tree ants move out, birds called trogons move in. These brightly colored rainforest birds from Africa, Asia, Central, and South America do not build their own nests. Instead, they dig holes in abandoned tree ants' nests and lay their eggs inside.

Orangutans are endangered because their forest homes are being chopped down.

These bats are white. But when the sun shines through their green tent walls, the bats take on a greenish tinge which hides them from enemies.

WHICH BATS MAKE TENTS?

One type of South American bat, the tent-making bat (*Ectophylla alba*), makes a tent-like shelter from a large leaf, with the leaf still attached to its tree. The bats chew away along either side of the leaf's mid-rib so that the leaf hangs down on either side—just like a tent! Then they spend the day roosting underneath, clinging on to the mid-rib with their claws.

WHERE DO GORILLAS SLEEP?

At night, a gorilla will find a safe place to sleep on the ground or in the trees. Then it builds itself a cosy bed from branches and leaves. This takes about five minutes. Then the gorilla snuggles down for a rest, pressing the bed into shape with its body. Gorillas live in tiny patches of rainforest in Africa.

WHO LIVES IN A TREEHOUSE AND EATS MONKEYS?

Giant eagles, such as the monkey-eating eagle of the Philippines and the South American harpy eagle, live high up in the tops of the emergent trees. They swoop through the canopy on the look-out for monkeys to eat. The eagles build huge twig platforms in the treetops where they lay their eggs. They use the same nest year after year.

WHICH BIRDS HANG THEIR NESTS FROM TREES?

In the rainforests of South America, oropendola birds build nests hanging from tree branches. One tree may be home to hundreds of birds. The nests look a bit like saggy string bags, over 3 feet long. The birds like to share their tree with bees, because the bees keep harmful flies away from their chicks.

WHICH INSECTS LIVE IN A TOWER?

Termites are tiny creatures, no bigger than grains of rice. They live in the rainforests of Africa, Asia, and South America, in huge groups many millions strong. Some termites build tower-like nests on the forest floor, made of chewed-up wood, glued together with spit. Others build their nests in trees.

A soldier termite stands on guard with its enormous head and jaws.

TERMITE

TOUCAN

Geckos often stick out their big, red tongues to scare attackers away!

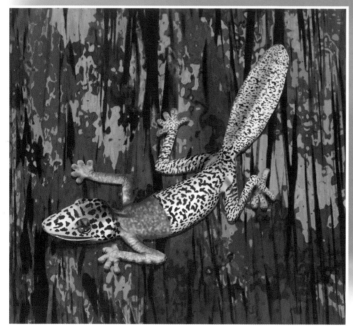

GECKO

WHAT MAKES A LEAF-TAILED GECKO INVISIBLE?

The leaf-tailed gecko of Madagascar spends the day head-down on a tree trunk. You might think that this would make it an easy target for enemies—but you'd be wrong! The gecko is superbly camouflaged. Its dappled green-brown skin matches the color of the bark perfectly. Its large, flat tail and ragged frill of skin make it look just like a woody bump.

WHAT DO KATYDIDS DO?

Katydids are small grasshoppers that disguise themselves brilliantly. Some look exactly like dead brown leaves, complete with holes, lying still on the forest floor of the rainforests of Asia and South America. Others mimic green, living leaves fluttering from a branch. They even have vein-like markings like real leaves.

WHY DO TIGERS HAVE STRIPES?

A tiger's stripes help to hide it among the undergrowth as it stalks or lies in wait for its prey. Its black and gold stripes break up the outline of its body, making it more difficult to see. Today, tigers are very rare. A very few still live in the rainforests of Asia.

WHICH ANIMAL CAN CHANGE COLOR?

Chameleons are masters of disguise. Their skin is usually green or brown but they can change color to blend in with their background or show that they are angry or frightened. They do this by enlarging or shrinking special color cells in their skin. Chameleons live in the rainforests of Asia and Africa.

Toucans live in the Amazon rainforest.

WHICH BUTTERFLIES KEEP VANISHING?

As a *Morpho* butterfly flies through the rainforest trees of South America, it seems to vanish, then reappear. This is because its wings are brilliant electric-blue on top and brown underneath. Each beat of its wings produces a flash, like a strobe light.

WHY DO TOUCANS HAVE SUCH COLORFUL BEAKS?

Toucans are famous for their striking beaks, which can grow longer than their bodies. They use their beaks for reaching over and plucking fruit from branches. The bright colors may help the toucans to recognize each other and to scare off other birds.

WHY DO SLOTHS HAVE GREEN FUR?

Sloths are so slow-moving that tiny green plants called algae grow on their coats. This helps to camouflage the sloth among the trees of the rainforests of Central and South America. The algae provides food for the moth caterpillars that also live happily on the sloth's fur.

WHICH RAINFOREST INSECT LOOKS LIKE A FLOWER?

In the rainforest, things aren't always what they seem. Many animals are cleverly disguised as twigs, leaves, bark, and even flowers. This hides them from hungry enemies and allows them to sneak up on prey unawares. The exquisite orchid mantis of Malaysia looks just like a beautiful flower. The mantis lurks on a twig, ready to shoot out its arms and grab interested insects.

WHAT WOULD HAPPEN IF YOU TROD ON A STINGRAY?

You'd get a painful shock! Stingrays are usually quite harmless unless you go and step on one. Sharp poisonous spines grow near the end of their long thin tails. If disturbed, a stingray whips its tail round and stabs the spine into its attacker. Stingrays live in the Amazon River in South America.

HOW DO ARROW-POISON FROGS GET THEIR NAME?

The brightly colored skin of a South American arrow-poison frog is a signal to would-be attackers. It warns them that the frog is very nasty indeed to eat. The frog's slimy skin is deadly poisonous. Forest people extract the poison and use it to tip their hunting arrows. And this is how arrow-poison frogs get their name.

WHICH SNAKE WAS ONCE USED AS A WEAPON?

The fer-de-lance is a deadly poisonous snake that grows up to 8 feet long. It is said that local people in South America used to slip these snakes into tubes and use them as lethal weapons to fire at their enemies.

WHICH ANIMAL HAS A STING IN ITS TAIL?

If you're out and about in rainforests all over the world, particularly at night, watch out for scorpions. They have a sting in their tails, loaded with deadly poison. A scorpion uses its tail mainly in self-defense, and holds it curled above its body, ready to strike.

Just one drop of this frog's poison is enough to kill a large bird almost instantly.

ARROW POISON FROG

WHICH ANIMAL SHOOTS BOILING POISON AT ITS ENEMIES?

Many rainforest beetles are poisonous, including bombardiers.

Bombardier beetles have a very unusual and unpleasant way of warning off enemies. When provoked, the beetle swivels the tip of its abdomen round and shoots a spray of boiling hot, poisonous chemicals at its attacker. The spray is made inside the beetle's body, from two otherwise quite harmless chemicals. They react together with an explosive sound loud enough for you to hear. There's no escape—the beetle has a very accurate aim!

ARE ANY BIRDS POISONOUS?

Until recently, scientists did not think so. Then, in 1992, it was found that the feathers and skin of the pitohui bird of Papua New Guinea contained a poison strong enough to kill mice and frogs. In people, it can cause numbness, burning, and sneezing.

DO CENTIPEDES HAVE A POISONOUS BITE?

Centipedes are fierce hunters and their first pair of legs is modified into fangs. These are used to inject poison into prey. Most centipedes are small and harmless to people. But large centipedes can pack an agonizingly painful bite. Centipedes live in rainforests all over the world.

WHICH SNAKE PRETENDS TO BE POISONOUS?

For some rainforest animals, pretending to be poisonous is the next best thing to being poisonous. In South America, harmless false coral snakes mimic the bright colors of extremely poisonous true coral snakes to trick their enemies into leaving them alone.

FER-DE-LANCE SNAKE

There are 2,700 types of snake, but only 400 are poisonous.

GIRAFFE-NECKED WEEVIL

WHICH BEETLE LOOKS LIKE A GIRAFFE?

The bizarre giraffe-necked weevil from Madagascar is one of the oddest-looking insects in the rainforest. Males have very long heads—about half the length of their bodies.

No one knows why this weevil has such a strange head.

WHICH IS THE SHYEST RAINFOREST ANIMAL?

The shyest animal in the rainforest is probably the okapi. These timid creatures are related to giraffes and look like a cross between a short-necked giraffe and a zebra. They live only in the rainforests of Zaire, Africa. Okapis are so secretive and solitary that, apart from local people, no one knew they even existed until 1901.

OKAPI

Okapis are endangered because their forest homes are being destroyed and they are poached for their meat.

WHAT KEEPS ITS BABY IN A WATERTIGHT POUCH?

The yapok is a marsupial from Central and South America that is adapted for life in water. It has webbed back feet to help it swim after its prey of fish, frogs, and crustaceans. Its pouch opens backward so that it stays watertight when the yapok dives into the water.

WHICH BUG HAS A LANTERN HEAD?

The lantern bug from South America got its name because people once thought that its odd-shaped head glowed in the dark. In fact, its large head looks a bit like a miniature crocodile. It may be useful for scaring off enemies and stopping the bug from being eaten.

HOW MANY MOUNTAIN GORILLAS ARE THERE?

There are three separate groups of mountain gorillas, all in the rainforests of Central Africa. All three are endangered because of forest clearance and poaching for their meat. Scientists estimate that there may be fewer than 40,000 left in the wild.

GOLDEN LION TAMARIN

Golden lion tamarins are illegally captured for the pet trade and zoos.

WHICH FLIES' EYES POP OUT ON STALKS?

Diopsid flies live in many rainforests. They have eyes on the end of long stalks. No one is quite sure why. One idea is that the stalks look like wasps' antennae. Predators mistake the flies for wasps, which might sting if they get any closer.

WHICH IS THE RAREST RAINFOREST ANIMAL?

So much of their forest home has been cleared to make space for coffee, rubber, and banana plantations that there may be fewer than 250 golden lion tamarins left in the wild. The last remaining tamarins live in a few patches of rainforest along the Atlantic coast of Brazil. Efforts are being made to save the tamarins. If these fail, they could be extinct within just a few years.

WHAT IS WHITE AND PINK AND KEEPS ITS BABY IN ITS POCKET?

A cuscus is a marsupial from Papua New Guinea. It has a pouch on its front where its young grow and develop. The cuscus has a thick white coat and a long tail with a bare pink tip. It uses its tail to help it climb through the trees.

Anacondas like to live in trees as well as in water.

ANACONDA

WHICH BIRD IS SMALLER THAN A BUTTERFLY?

The bee hummingbird of South America is the world's smallest bird. It measures just over 2 inches in length, nearly half of which is its bill and tail. This tiny creature is smaller than many of the butterflies and moths in its rainforest home.

WHICH IS THE BIGGEST RAINFOREST SNAKE?

The gigantic anaconda of South America is the world's biggest snake. The heaviest on record was 27 feet long, more than 3 feet round its middle and weighed almost a quarter of a ton. Anacondas lurk in the water at the river's edge, with just their eyes and nostrils showing, waiting for their prey. They can kill prey as large as deer, goats, and alligators, crushing them to death with their huge coils.

WHICH BIRD BUILDS THE SMALLEST NESTS?

The vervain hummingbird of South America builds a nest from plants and cobwebs that's only about the size of half a walnut shell. There it lays the smallest eggs of any bird, barely the size of peas. The bee hummingbird's nest is also tiny, about the size of a thimble.

ARE BIG ANIMALS THE MOST DANGEROUS?

No, they're not! The most dangerous animals are small insects—mosquitoes. They spread malaria, a disease that kills millions of people a year. Symptoms include a raging fever. Mosquitoes can also pass on yellow fever and elephantiasis. They live in rainforests all over the world.

WHICH ANIMAL HAS THE BIGGEST APPETITE?

You might think that the answer would be a jaguar or an alligator. In fact, it's the larva of the polyphemus moth, which lives in Central America. It eats a staggering 86,000 times its own birth weight in food in the first two days of its life!

THREE-TOED SLOTH

WHICH IS THE LAZIEST RAINFOREST ANIMAL?

The laziest animal in the rainforest has to be the three-toed sloth from South America. This idle animal spends about 18 hours a day hanging upside down from a tree branch, fast asleep. It spends the rest of the time looking for food. Unusually, its shaggy hair also grows upside down, from its belly toward its back. This is so that the rain runs off it more easily and the sleepy sloth does not get waterlogged!

WHICH RODENT BREAKS RECORDS?

The world's biggest rodent is the capybara from South America. (Rodents are animals such as mice and rats.) It's about the size of a pig and lives around lakes, rivers, and marshes. Its arch enemy is the jaguar, the fiercest hunter in the rainforest.

WHICH SPIDER IS AS BIG AS A PLATE?

Including its eight hairy legs, a bird-eating spider, or tarantula, can grow as big as a plate. It's the biggest spider in the world and lives in South America. Bird-eating spiders hunt at night, on the rainforest floor. Despite their name, they very rarely catch birds.

The three-toed sloth even eats its food hanging upside down.

SECTION SEVEN

LIFE IN THE FROZEN WASTES

The Arctic fox keeps warm with the help of its thick fur coat and a layer of body fat.

ARCTIC FOX

HOW DO ARCTIC FOXES KEEP THEIR NOSES WARM AT NIGHT?

The Arctic fox has a bushy tail up to 16 inches long—over half its body length. When the fox is sleeping, it curls its tail around its body to cover its head and nose. The tail acts as a muff to keep the animal snug in biting winds.

HOW CAN ANIMALS SURVIVE THE HARSH POLAR WEATHER?

The polar regions are the coldest places on earth, yet some creatures live there all year round. Snow and ice cover the land and sea for most or all of the year. Summers are brief and cool, with long hours of daylight. Winters are long, dark, and bitterly cold. In the Arctic, mammals such as the wolf and Arctic fox have a layer of body fat and a thick coat of fur to keep them warm. The fur traps air next to the animal's skin, which helps to prevent body heat from escaping.

WHICH ANIMAL HAS EARS ADAPTED TO KEEP IT WARM?

In hot places such as deserts, hares have very long ears which give off body heat to keep the animal cool. In the far north, Arctic hares have much shorter ears which release less heat, while still giving excellent hearing.

HOW DO BIRDS KEEP WARM IN THE POLAR REGIONS?

Birds that live in the Arctic and Antarctic all year round have a dense coat of feathers. Waterproof outer feathers protect the bird against the cold and wet. Underneath, soft, fluffy down feathers help retain body heat.

HOW DO SEALS KEEP WARM IN ICY WATER?

Seals and walruses are mammals that spend most of their lives in cold water. They have a thick layer of fat called blubber below their skin. This fatty layer keeps them warm and well insulated in the water. Whales and polar bears also have blubber. Whale blubber can be up to 20 inches thick.

HOW DO POLAR ANIMALS AVOID FROZEN FEET?

An animal's feet can be one of the coldest parts of its body, especially when, as in the polar regions, the feet touch the ice or frozen soil. Mammals such as polar bears and Arctic foxes have hair between their toes to prevent their paws from freezing. Some polar birds, such as the ptarmigan, a type of grouse, have feathery feet for the same reason.

HARP SEAL

The harp seal's blubber keeps it warm in cold water.

One guillemot threatens another by spreading its wings and pointing skyward with its beak. Its opponent backs down by preening its feathers or bowing with outstretched wings.

WHAT IS A BEACHMASTER?

Southern elephant seals breed on islands off Antarctica. Rival males fight fiercely, rearing up and tearing at each other's necks with their teeth. The seals' necks are padded with thick skin and fat, but the animals are soon bloody. The victor becomes "beachmaster," winning a stretch of beach and his own group, or "harem" of females.

WHAT MAKES POLAR BEARS FIGHT?

Polar bears live mostly solitary lives, roaming the lonely pack ice. Females breed only once every three years. If two male bears come across a female who is ready to mate, a fight breaks out. The males wrestle fiercely in the snow, for only the victor will get the chance to mate.

Rival male elephant seals battle each other to become "beachmaster."

ELEPHANT SEALS

WHAT BIRD DANCES TO ATTRACT A MATE?

Sandhill cranes migrate to the Arctic to breed. The male and female birds court one another by performing "dances" with many different steps. The birds dip down and bow low, make skipping movements, and leap up to 20 feet in the air.

WHICH PENGUIN FLIRTS WITH ITS EYEBROWS?

Rockhopper penguins have tufts of feathers above their eyes that form spectacular "eyebrows." Males and females court by squawking at one another and waggling their heads to show off their impressive tufts.

HOW DO GUILLEMOTS KEEP THE PEACE?

Guillemots rear their chicks on crowded cliff ledges. Each breeding pair has only a tiny space to feed its chick. In these overcrowded conditions, fights between rival birds would quickly lead to chicks or eggs falling to their deaths. Squabbling guillemots resolve their differences by using ritual movements that show threat and submission, so physical fights are rare.

WHAT MAKES A WOLF LEADER OF THE PACK?

Wolf packs have a strict system, in which the strongest animals dominate the weaker ones. Only the strongest male and female wolf usually mate. Whenever they meet, wolves show their place in the hierarchy through their body language. Top wolves stand proud with pricked ears, bared teeth, and tails held high. Junior wolves cower with their ears flat and their tails between their legs.

Polar bear cubs spend two years suckling their mother's milk and learning hunting skills. Then they are on their own.

POLAR BEAR CUBS

WHAT GAMES DO POLAR BEAR CUBS PLAY?

Young polar bears are curious and very playful. They chase one another, slide down snowy slopes, and tussle in the snow. Through play, they learn the skills they will need to survive once they are weaned.

WHERE ARE POLAR BEAR CUBS BORN?

Polar bears give birth in midwinter to up to three cubs. The young are born in a snug snow den hollowed out by their mother. They live in the den for three months, feeding on her rich milk. Then the female breaks through the snow plugging the entrance to the den, and the cubs scamper out into the icy world for the first time.

WHY DO BRANT GEESE RAISE THEIR YOUNG IN A HURRY?

Brant geese arrive to breed in Arctic marshes as soon as the ice melts. The young must be raised before the brief summer ends, so the birds lay their eggs at once. The eggs hatch out quickly, and the chicks grow fast. In less than two months the young birds are ready to take off with their parents as they head back to warmer climes.

Young Brant geese learn to swim soon after they hatch out.

WHICH ANIMAL DRINKS MILK UNDERWATER?

Like other mammals, young whales feed on their mothers' milk. The female's nipples are located on the underside of her body, so the calf must take a deep breath and dive down below its mother to drink.

A blue whale calf drinks 175 pints of its mother's milk a day.

BLUE WHALES

WHICH CHICKS ARE LOOKED AFTER IN A CRECHE?

Emperor penguin chicks hatch out in July—midwinter in Antarctica. They spend about eight weeks riding round on their parents' feet, clear of the ice. Then they are left in "creches" with other young penguins while their parents go off to hunt for food.

WHICH ANIMAL CAN WALK A GREAT DISTANCE AT ONLY TWO DAYS OLD?

Caribou calves are born in June in the Arctic. In minutes, they are able to stand on their long legs and wobble around. In a day or two, they are ready to keep up with the herd as it moves on in search of fresh grazing. In the fall, the calves travel south with the herd to the sheltered forests.

WHAT ANIMAL HAS SEVERAL DENS?

Ringed seal pups are born in an ice den scraped out by their mother with her flippers. The female makes several dens so she can move her pup to safety if it is threatened. Polar bear cubs spend two years suckling their mother's milk and learning hunting skills. Then they are on their own.

BRANT GEESE

HOW DO BABY SEALS MAKE THEMSELVES INVISIBLE?

Baby harp seals spend the first weeks of their lives out of water, on the ice. Their parents have dark, mottled skins that blend in well with the water, but the young have pure white fur, which helps to hide them from predators such as polar bears.

SNOWY OWLS

Snowy owls feed their chicks on lemmings and other small mammals.

HOW DOES THE SNOWY OWL PROTECT ITS BABIES?

Snowy owl chicks hatch out in a nest on the ground in springtime. The young and adult owls have different camouflage. The mother owl has white feathers with dark speckles, so she blends into the snowy landscape. Her chicks have mottled gray feathers that merge with rocks and plants near the nest.

WHAT COLOR IS A POLAR BEAR'S SKIN?

Believe it or not, the polar bear's skin is black! The hollow hairs of its thick fur reflect the light and make its skin look white.

REINDEER HERD

HOW DO REINDEER ESCAPE THE WINTER COLD?

Some hardy animals can survive in the high Arctic all year round. Others, including reindeer, visit only for the mild summer season. Reindeer herds spend the summer months feeding on small plants in the tundra—the treeless lands on the edge of the Arctic Ocean. In fall, they make their way south, to shelter for the winter in forests called the taiga. The reindeer make the same round trip each year, following the same routes. Such regular animal journeys are called migrations.

WHAT ARCTIC ANIMAL HAS TWO FUR COATS?

The stoat is a type of weasel whose camouflage varies with the seasons. In summer its brown fur blends in with the rocky landscape. In fall it sheds its summer fur, and grows a new, thick coat of pure white hairs. In its winter coat the stoat is called an ermine.

HOW DO POLAR ANIMALS PERFORM A DISAPPEARING ACT?

Animals all over the world have colors and patterns on their bodies that blend in with their surroundings. This natural disguise or camouflage helps them to hide from enemies and predators. In the Arctic and Antarctic, many creatures have white coats that blend in with the snow in winter. Some creatures have a different colored coat in summer, so they can also hide when the snow has melted. In winter, the ptarmigan has mainly snow-white feathers. In summer, its mottled brown plumage helps it hide among the bare earth and rocks.

WHY DO REINDEER FOLLOW IN EACH OTHER'S FOOTSTEPS?

Reindeer travel as much as 1,240 miles each year on migration. To save energy, each deer treads in the footsteps of the animal in front, so it does not have to break trail through deep snow.

Long lines of migrating reindeer stretch for 185 miles or more, as the animals make their way through the barren wastes and across mighty rivers.

HOW DOES THE LYNX GO HUNTING?

Like other cats, the lynx has excellent sight and hearing. It hunts by silently stalking a victim such as an Arctic hare. Then it pounces on its prey with one big leap.

The lynx's camouflaged coat allows it to creep up on victims.

WHICH ANIMAL HAS PAWS LIKE SLEDGEHAMMERS?

The polar bear's main weapons are its paws, which can act like sledgehammers. It can kill a human with one swipe of its massive paw. The bear's sharp canine teeth are also sometimes used to kill. Its strongest senses are smell and hearing. A hunting bear can sense prey up to 20 miles away.

WHICH ANIMALS FORM A MAGIC CIRCLE ROUND THEIR BABIES?

When musk oxen are menaced by wolves or other predators, they group themselves into a circle with their young calves safe in the middle. The adult oxen face outward and fend off their attackers with their long, curving horns, until the wolves give up.

WHICH ANIMAL KEEPS FOOD IN A "FRIDGE?"

Arctic foxes sometimes cache (hide) stores of meat beneath the snow, or under rocks in summer. In cold conditions, the food stays as fresh as it would in the icebox of your fridge.

WHAT DO POLAR BEARS EAT?

The polar bear's favorite food is ringed seals. It hunts its victims at holes in the ice where the seals come up for air. The bear creeps silently up to the hole, then lies in wait—for hours if necessary. When a seal pops up to breathe, the bear kills it with a single slash of its powerful paw and a bite to the neck.

The wolverine sometimes steals prey killed by other Arctic hunters. It is so fierce that the other predator just gives up its kill.

WHICH ANIMALS GANG UP ON THEIR VICTIMS?

Wolves' main prey are caribou, moose, and sometimes musk oxen. They hunt in packs and target young, weak, or injured animals. When the wolves spot a likely victim, such as a caribou calf with its mother, they spread out to surround their prey. The panicked calf tries to flee and is separated from its mother. Then the wolves run their victim down and kill it by biting its neck.

WHAT ANIMAL IS THE GLUTTON OF THE ARCTIC?

Wolverines are large members of the weasel family, also known as gluttons. These ferocious creatures look like small brown bears. They hunt lemmings and even large mammals such as reindeer. When the wolverine makes a large kill, it gorges itself on meat, then hides the rest for later, earning a reputation for gluttony.

WOLVERINE

WHAT ARCTIC ANIMAL WAS THOUGHT TO COMMIT SUICIDE?

Lemmings were once believed to commit suicide by throwing themselves off cliffs. Now scientists realize that these rodents breed very fast, so their numbers can rise steeply. When the area where they live becomes overcrowded and food gets scarce, large numbers of lemmings set off in search of a new food source. Many of them drown when they fall into rivers or lakes that lie in their path.

WHEN DO GRIZZLIES GO NORTH?

The polar bear is the only bear to spend all year on the Arctic pack ice. However, grizzly bears live in the forests that edge the tundra. In summer, they visit the Arctic to feed on berries, fish, and mammals. They pass the winter hibernating in dens.

ARE THERE CATS IN THE ARCTIC?

The lynx is a large wild cat that spends most of the year in the taiga forests. It sometimes ventures into the Arctic tundra to hunt hares, voles, and lemmings.

WHICH ARCTIC ANIMAL MAKES THE SCARIEST NOISE?

The eerie noise that wolves make has been used in many horror films!

Wolves are found throughout the Arctic, living in packs. Most wolf packs contain between eight and 20 animals. They howl to communicate with other members of their group, and to warn rival wolves away from their territory.

WHAT DO CARIBOU LIKE TO EAT?

Caribou is a type of deer that feeds mainly on lichen growing on rocks. This is a food that can be found all year round. In summer, the deer feed on a wide variety of plants that grow and flourish in the long hours of daylight.

The polar bear's scientific name, Ursus maritimus, means "sea bear." These mammals are often classed as sea creatures.

POLAR BEAR

WOLF

HOW BIG DO POLAR BEARS GROW?

Male polar bears can grow up to 10 feet long and weigh as much as 10 adult humans. The females are much smaller.

WHICH ANIMAL IS A CHAMPION SWIMMER?

Polar bears are expert swimmers and divers. They move through the water by paddling with their front paws. They have been spotted swimming as far as 200 miles from land.

WHAT IS THE MOST FAMOUS ARCTIC ANIMAL?

Rudolf, the red-nosed reindeer who pulled Santa's sleigh, is certainly the best-loved Arctic animal! In Siberia and Scandinavia, tame reindeer are often used to pull sleighs and heavy loads, and people also ride on them. Throughout the Arctic, humans depend on reindeer for meat and use their skins for clothing. In North America, reindeer are sometimes called caribou. The name probably comes from a Micmac Indian word meaning "animal that paws through snow for food."

MARBLE PLUNDERFISH

The marble plunderfish uses the fleshy barbel on its chin like a fisherman's bait, to catch smaller fish.

WHY DO FISH NEED ANTIFREEZE?

Fish that live in polar seas have special features that help them survive in icy water. The Arctic cod has blood that contains chemicals that work like the antifreeze in a car radiator, to prevent the fish from freezing.

WHICH ANTARCTIC FISH GOES FISHING?

The marble plunder fish has a fleshy whisker on its chin, called a barbel. To small fish, this slender tentacle looks like a wriggling worm. But when the little fish moves in to eat the "worm," the plunder fish snaps it up.

The icefish has pale, nearly see-through skin.

ICEFISH

HOW DOES THE ICEFISH GET ITS NAME?

Icefish can survive in very cold water, where most other fish would freeze. Unlike all other vertebrates (animals with backbones) the icefish's blood contains no red blood cells; instead, it holds a natural antifreeze. Red blood cells are normally vital because they carry oxygen round an animal's body, but the icefish can absorb oxygen direct from seawater.

WHY DO POLAR SEA CREATURES PREFER THE DEEP?

Most aquatic animals in polar seas live in deep water. In shallow waters, creatures that live on the seabed risk damage from floating sea-ice that scrapes along the bottom. So starfish, sponges, corals, and sea-urchins carpet the rocky bottom of the deep water. When the ice melts in summer, some of these creatures migrate inshore.

WHY ARE THE POLAR SEAS A POPULAR PLACE TO LIVE?

In the polar regions, far more creatures live in the oceans than on land. In winter, the sea surface freezes over, but under the ice, the water temperature is warmer than the air on land. Antarctic waters contain an even greater variety of life than Arctic waters, because the ocean currents there cause nourishing minerals to well up from deep waters, to feed sea creatures.

WHEN DOES A SEA SNAIL DRY OUT?

Some Antarctic sea snails survive the cold by dehydrating (drying out) so the water in their body cells cannot freeze.

WAS THE ANTARCTIC ONCE A WARM SEA?

Fossil remains of ancient warm-water dwellers such as ammonites (shelled creatures) show that the Antarctic was much warmer in prehistoric times. Ammonites were related to squid. They have long since become extinct.

Greenland sharks can grow up to 20 feet long.

WHICH SHARKS LIKE TO CHILL OUT IN THE ARCTIC?

Most sharks live in warm or temperate waters. Greenland sharks visit Arctic seas, although they usually live in warmer, deeper waters further south. These sharks hunt squid, seals, and small whales.

GREENLAND SHARK

WHICH SEAL HAS A BEARD?

The bearded seal has a magnificent set of long, whiskery hairs on its nose. It uses its sensitive "beard" to feel for shellfish lurking on the seabed and fish hiding in cloudy water.

Leopard seals are fast movers, like the big cats after which they are named.

LEOPARD SEAL

HOW DO LEOPARD SEALS HUNT PENGUINS?

The leopard seal lurks beneath an ice floe on which the birds are standing. When the penguins dive into the sea, the seal darts forward and seizes a bird in its teeth. Having caught its prey, the leopard is in no hurry to feed. It beats its kill against the water to turn the penguin inside-out and remove its skin. It may take over an hour to finish its meal.

WHICH SEAL NEEDS A NEW NAME?

Crabeater seals of the Antarctic do not eat crabs. They would be better renamed krill-eaters, as these small, shrimp-like animals are their main food. To catch krill, the seal speeds along with its mouth open, sieving krill from the water with the help of its jagged teeth.

DO ELEPHANT SEALS HAVE TRUNKS?

Male elephant seals have a wrinkled bag of skin on top of their nose. The bag can be blown up balloon-style, to form a kind of trunk. When inflated, the seal's trunk acts as a loudspeaker, amplifying his roars as he calls to frighten off rival males.

WHY DO WALRUSES HAVE TUSKS?

Both male and female walruses have sharp, curving tusks up to 3 feet long. These strong, elongated upper teeth have many uses. Walruses eat clams and other shellfish, and use their tusks to rake along the seabed to find food. The tusks are also used as levers when walruses haul their massive bodies up on to the ice. Long, curving tusks may add sex appeal when walruses are courting. The males also use theirs to gore their rivals when fighting contests to win female partners.

WALRUS

WHEN IS A SEAL AN ELEPHANT?

The elephant seal is the heavyweight champion of the seal world. Large males may grow up to 21 feet long and weigh up to 8,800 lb. Females are much smaller. Southern elephant seals live in Antarctic waters.

DO WALRUSES LIKE TO PARTY?

Yes! Walruses are very sociable animals. They often gather in large, noisy groups on land, basking in the sun or huddling together to conserve body heat in cold weather. The walrus pack provides safety in numbers because it is more difficult for enemies to pick out weak or young animals from a big group.

The walrus' name comes from a Swedish word meaning "whale-horse."

WHERE DO PENGUINS LIVE?

Penguins live only in the Southern Hemisphere. There are 16 different species. Most live in the far south, in Antarctica, or on islands in the south Pacific or Atlantic Oceans. A few species occur further north, and one even lives on the remote Galapagos Islands, near the equator.

WHY IS A PENGUIN LIKE A CORK?

To leave the water, penguins swim up to the shore at speed, and then pop out of the water like a cork from a bottle, to land on the ice feet first. They sometimes use this technique to escape from predators, such as leopard seals.

Seven species of penguin live in Antarctica.

WHEN IS A PENGUIN LIKE A TOBOGGAN?

On land, penguins walk with an ungainly waddle. When descending snowy slopes, they toboggan along on their stomachs, pushing with their feet for extra speed.

WHICH PENGUIN IS THE DEEPEST DIVER?

The emperor penguin can dive to depths of 870 feet, and stay below the surface for 18 minutes. The emperor is the largest penguin, growing up to 4 feet tall.

HOW DID CHINSTRAP AND ADELIE PENGUINS GET THEIR NAMES?

The chinstrap penguin has a narrow line of black feathers running under its white throat, like a chinstrap. Adelie penguins were named by the French explorer Dumont d'Urville, who discovered Antarctica in 1840, after his wife Adelie.

ADELIE PENGUINS

HOW DO PENGUINS KEEP WARM?

In the harsh Antarctic climate, penguins keep warm with the help of a layer of fatty blubber, and two layers of feathers. Their outer coat of tiny oily feathers overlap to keep the down feathers below dry. Penguins also have partly feathered beaks and small feet, so only a small part of their body is exposed to the freezing air and ice.

WHY DO PENGUINS STEAL PEBBLES?

Penguins breed in large, noisy colonies called rookeries. Some make no nests, but chinstrap and Adelie penguins build nests of pebbles. Aggressive chinstraps sometimes steal one another's pebbles, or take over Adelie nests.

CAN PENGUINS FLY?

Penguins are flightless birds, but they are strong swimmers and divers. Underwater, they "fly" along, using their wings as flippers to push against the water. When swimming at speed, they often leap out of the water and dive back in again, an action known as porpoising.

HOW DO EMPERORS KEEP THEIR EGGS WARM?

Emperor penguins don't build nests, and an egg left on the ice would freeze in seconds. The female lays her egg, the male scoops it up onto his feet, and covers it with a warm flap of skin. He incubates the egg for two months during the worst winter weather, until the female returns to help feed the newly-hatched chick.

Out on the windy pack ice, male emperor penguins incubate their eggs.

WHICH PENGUIN LAYS ITS EGGS ON ICE?

Most Antarctic penguins breed on land in summer, but emperor penguins breed in winter; out on the freezing ice. In April, they trek 60 miles to traditional nesting sites, where they mate. Then the females head back to the sea, and the males are left to incubate the eggs.

EMPEROR PENGUIN

SECTION EIGHT

VANISHING LIFE

WHERE DO GIANT PANDAS LIVE?

In bamboo forests in China. Once they were seen all over this vast country, but sadly today they can be found in only three small provinces in western China. Red pandas are more adaptable to habitat and can be found in China and other parts of Asia, including the Himalayas.

HOW LONG DOES A PANDA TAKE TO EAT LUNCH?

Almost all its waking hours! Giant pandas spend around 14 hours every day eating. An adult panda will eat up to 66 lb of bamboo in a day—this is one third of its body weight! The reason they need to eat so much is because bamboo has very little nutritional value.

WHICH ANIMAL IS ALL THUMBS?

Giant pandas have an extra "finger" in their front paws. It is where a human's little finger would be and works similarly to the thumb. This gives the panda the power of two thumbs, so it can grip its food while eating.

WHAT IS THREATENING THE GIANT PANDA?

The shortage of bamboo, which is the panda's food. Bamboo forests are very delicate. Bamboo does not keep growing like other forest plants. When it flowers, it dies. If the bamboo in one forest is all of the same age, the whole forest will die at the same time. All the pandas living in that forest will then starve. Humans are the pandas' biggest enemies, because they have taken their land and hunted them. It is now illegal in China to harm a panda in any way, and traders risk the death penalty.

The giant panda has special cheek teeth for crushing and slicing plant food.

GIANT PANDA

RED PANDA

HOW MANY GIANT PANDAS ARE LEFT IN THE WORLD?

There are believed to be fewer than 1,000 giant pandas left in the wild. Since 1974 their bamboo forests have died out at an alarming rate: in just 14 years half the forests died. Since then conservationists have been working tirelessly to preserve the pandas' habitat.

HOW OFTEN DO GIANT PANDAS HAVE BABIES?

Their cubs are born only every two years, at the most. This is another reason why giant pandas are endangered, especially as many cubs die shortly after birth. Cubs are born blind and without teeth, making them entirely dependent on their mothers.

HOW MANY TYPES OF PANDA ARE THERE?

The giant panda has one other panda relation—the red panda. Red pandas are much smaller and used to be thought of as not a panda at all, but a type of raccoon. They live in trees, have long, striped tails, and thin, cat-like faces with pointed ears. Their red fur has paler markings. Red pandas are often hunted, and some are captured alive to be sold as pets.

The red panda eats bamboo, roots, and some small animals.

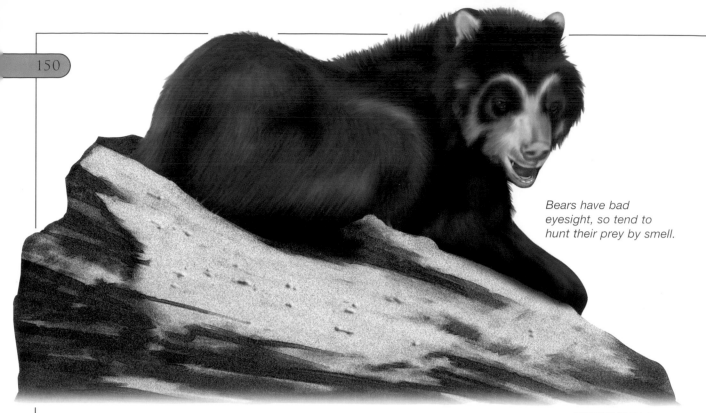

Bears have bad eyesight, so tend to hunt their prey by smell.

SPECTACLED BEAR

DO BEARS REALLY LIKE HONEY?

Yes they do. Many bears are expert climbers, and with their excellent sense of smell, finding a bee's nest is easy for them. Bears are omnivorous, which means they eat both meat and vegetation. They like eating other mammals, insects (even wasps, bees, and termites, whose stings seem not to bother them), plants, nuts, fish, eggs, fruit, and people's picnic—if they can find them. They will also eat carrion (rotting meat) if necessary.

ARE POLAR BEARS ENDANGERED?

Polar bears live in the Arctic, the area around the North Pole. They live in the mountains and lowland, in areas where food is plentiful, but they are endangered by hunters who are after polar bear skin and meat. The other species of bear are found all over North and South America, parts of Europe, and Asia.

WHY ARE BEARS HUNTED?

For their bones, bile, and gall bladders, which are made into traditional medicine, and for their fur. Bear meat is also eaten, in particular their paws. And there are still people who hunt bears as "trophies" for sport. Most cruelly, bears are trapped to be used as dancing bears or for bear baiting.

WHICH BEARS ARE MOST ENDANGERED?

The most endangered bear in the world is the giant panda, although all species of brown bear, polar bear, and black bear are killed for their fur and are under threat from fur hunters.

WHICH IS THE BIGGEST BEAR?

The biggest bear in the world is the endangered kodiak bear, a member of the brown bear species. It lives in Alaska and stands up to 10 feet tall. It can weigh up to 704 lb.

KODIAK BEAR

The kodiak bear is a type of grizzly bear.

WHEN IS A BROWN BEAR BLUE?

Not counting pandas, there are seven species of bear: the American black bear, Asian black bear, brown bear, polar bear, sloth bear, spectacled bear, and sun bear. These names are very misleading. For instance, a brown bear's coat can range in color from cream to very dark brown, and it can also look gray-blue! Black bears can also be brown and, to most people who aren't experts, two bears of the same species can look very different from one another.

WHY DO BEARS HIBERNATE?

They sleep all winter because food is scarce. In summer a bear will eat continually, storing up fat to use for energy during the winter. Females need to store up especially large fat reserves as their cubs are born during hibernation and need to be fed with rich milk.

DO BEARS LIKE FISH?

Yes, fish makes up a large part of their diet in parts of the world where rivers are plentiful. In North America, Alaska, and Canada bears can often be seen skilfully catching enormous salmon.

GRIZZLY BEAR

WHY IS A GRIZZLY BEAR GRIZZLY?

A grizzly is actually one of the many different types of brown bear. The word grizzly comes from the french word *gris*, meaning gray. When the sun catches a grizzly bear's fur, the tips of the hairs look as if they are tinged with gray.

WHY ARE GORILLAS ENDANGERED?

Gorillas live in Africa—in Zaire, Rwanda, and Uganda—in mountainous areas and in the lowland rainforests. In 1925, their mountain home was made the first national park in Africa. Sadly, Zaire, Rwanda, and Uganda have suffered severely over the last few decades, experiencing terrifying wars, droughts, and famines. This has caused terrible devastation to the gorilla population as well as to the human world. All gorillas are endangered.

ARE WE RELATED TO GORILLAS?

Yes. Gorillas and humans have a common ancestor. This creature lived on earth many millions of years ago. The descendants of our common ancestor started two separate families, or evolutionary lines. One became human, the other became the ancestor of gorillas. Like humans, gorillas are a member of the Primate order. Within this order, both humans and gorillas are members of a scientific family called *Hominoidea*.

WHAT DO GORILLAS NEED FROM THEIR HABITAT?

Shelter and a good supply of food. If the climate is favorable, both mountain and lowland habitats can provide a gorilla family with all the food and nutrients they need. Mountain gorillas are severely endangered. Gorillas are mainly vegetarian and their habitats are rich in lush vegetation, as well as plentiful insects.

WHAT IS LIFE LIKE IN A GORILLA GROUP?

Gorilla society is run by male gorillas—it is called a patriarchal society, from the Latin word for father. The leader of the group is always a silverback (a mature male). Males often fight to show who is boss, and the loser must leave the group or be killed. Those that leave will often set up a new group of females and young.

HOW DO GORILLAS COMMUNICATE?

They use body signals and noises—perhaps the most famous of these is the male's habit of standing on his hind legs and beating his chest when angry. They play together, which teaches their young vital skills for survival.

WHY ARE GORILLAS HUNTED?

Tragically, one of the most common reasons they are hunted is as "trophies." Gorillas' skulls, hands, and feet are sold as souvenirs, just as elephant feet were in the 19th century. Gorillas have also been hunted for their meat, particularly during the famine that gripped Rwanda in the 1980s and 1990s.

HOW TALL IS A GORILLA?

A female gorilla stands at about 4 feet on her hind legs. A silverback male can reach up to 7 feet, although the average height of a male is 5 feet 6 inches. Males are called "silverbacks" when hair on their backs turns silver in mature adulthood.

SILVERBACK GORILLA

WHO TRIED TO SAVE THE GORILLAS?

Dr Dian Fossey was the gorillas' most famous helper. She spent much of her life trying to stop gorillas being captured or killed for trade. Sadly she was murdered in 1985. Since Dian Fossey's death, many action groups have continued her work. The story of her life was made into a film, *Gorillas In The Mist*.

WHAT HAPPENS TO GORILLAS IN WARTIME?

Gorillas are often innocent victims of fierce fighting. Occasionally, they get caught in the crossfire. Hungry troops may also track down a gorilla and kill it for food. As there are very few gorillas left in the world, killing even one could contribute to the extinction of the species.

Gorillas are the most intelligent animals next to human beings.

COYOTE

A coyote's howl can be heard several miles away.

IN WHAT COUNTRIES DO WOLVES, FOXES, AND WILD DOGS LIVE?

In every continent. There are wolves in Eastern Europe and Asia, jackals in Africa, coyotes in America, and dingoes in Australia. From the black-backed jackal in Africa to the gray wolf in Europe, many wolves are under threat. The wolves hunt in packs and kill their own prey as well as scavenging on dead animals. All wolves are disliked by farmers!

ARE WEREWOLVES EXTINCT?

No! They never existed. A werewolf is an imaginary beast—supposedly a human who can change into a wolf and attack other humans and animals. In folklore, this change takes place at the full moon—when people believe there is more crime and madness. Werewolves remain an important part of traditional storytelling, particularly in Eastern Europe, where there are many people who still believe werewolves exist.

DOES A FOX CUB MAKE A GOOD PET?

No wild animal should be kept as a pet. It takes many generations of breeding to completely tame any species. A fox cub may seem very playful and friendly, but its wild instincts would soon take over. No other pets, such as cats or rabbits, would be safe from it, and it could also attack humans, even those it knew well, through fear.

Jackals like to feed on fruit, small mammals, and even the bodies of larger animals that have died.

WHAT BONES ARE USED IN FOLK MEDICINE?

Conservationists are trying to stop canines being killed for their fur, and for parts of their bodies used in traditional medicines. In Africa, the simien jackal is hunted for its beautiful coat, and in South America the maned wolf is hunted for its bones. When powdered, the bones are believed to cure a variety of ills.

ARE THERE WOLVES IN AUSTRALIA?

Yes, but maybe not for long. The Tasmanian wolf used to live happily in Australia, but conservationists haven't spotted one for well over ten years, so they are beginning to become concerned that it has been hunted to extinction.

WHEN DID WOLVES BECOME EXTINCT IN BRITAIN?

Once Britain was almost covered in dense forest. When people began cutting it down, they destroyed the wolves' habitat and source of food—making wolves hungry and dangerous. The last wolf killed in Britain was in Scotland, in 1743. Ireland's last wolf perished about 50 years before, and in England, wolves were extinct by 1500.

SIMIEN JACKAL

Rhinos have a very good sense of smell and good hearing.

JAVAN RHINOCEROS

HOW MANY RHINOS ARE THERE LEFT IN THE WORLD?

There are less than 8,500 white rhinos still living. Almost all of these are southern whites, so the northern white rhinos are extremely endangered. There are around 2,600 black rhinos; 2,050 Indian rhinos; about 400 Sumatran rhinos; and—most endangered of all—only around 70 Javan rhinos left.

WHAT IS BEING DONE TO HELP RHINOS?

Where rhinos are found there are also specially trained guards. Obviously they can't be with the animals all the time, but they track them and make sure they know where the groups are. In many parts of the world, conservationists tranquilize rhinos and saw off their horns. This is not painful—it is like us cutting our hair or nails. Conservationists hope that if a rhino has no horn, the poachers will not kill it.

The black rhinoceros has no hair on its body and a very thick skin or hide.

DOES THE RHINO HAVE ANY EXTINCT RELATIONS?

There are five species of rhino: white, black, Sumatran, Javan, and Indian and they are all endangered. Thousands and thousands of years ago the rhino had a great many more relations—there was even a woolly rhino, with a similar coat to the woolly mammoth—but these are all now extinct.

WHERE DO RHINOS LIVE?

White and black rhinos live all over Africa. The Javan, Sumatran, and Indian rhinos, as their names suggest, live in Java, Sumatra, and India, all countries in Asia. Rhinos are also kept in zoos and safari parks all over the world. Many wildlife sanctuaries have set up rhinoceros breeding programs, hoping to help save the species from extinction.

BLACK RHINOCEROS

WHAT IS HAPPENING TO THE RHINOS' HABITAT?

Many Asian rhinos are endangered because their habitat—the rainforest—has been cut down for timber. This is a worldwide problem, as most rainforest countries are also poor countries that need to sell their resources. In Africa, the savanna (grassland) where the rhinos live is often under threat of drought.

WHAT IS THE RHINO'S BIGGEST ENEMY?

Big cats prey on rhinos, but they kill only a few. Humans are the reason rhinos are endangered. As well as poachers wanting their horn, farmers often shoot rhinos to stop them eating or trampling the crops. Previously, rhinos were also shot as "trophies" by big-game hunters.

WHY ARE RHINOS IN DANGER OF EXTINCTION?

Because there are so few rhinos left in the world, that just a few more years of hunting could wipe them out. An added danger is the sinister fact that when something is in short supply it always becomes more valuable—some poachers want to kill all rhinos just to make the rhino horn they own even more valuable.

WHICH CATS ARE THE BIG CATS?

Lions, tigers, cheetahs, leopards (including panthers), cougars (also called pumas), and jaguars are all big cats and animals from each group are endangered. There are also medium-sized cats, such as ocelots and lynxes that are endangered. These are too big to be counted as wild cats, but too small to be called big cats. Both the Texas ocelot and the Spanish lynx are endangered.

Leopards often live close to towns and villages.

ARE BIG CATS RELATED TO DOMESTIC CATS?

Yes, they are. All cats are of the order *Carnivora* (meat-eaters) and the family *Felidae* (felines). The domestic tabby has much in common with the tiger and its large relations. They hunt in similar ways and they all eat meat, but unlike their larger relations, they are not endangered.

WHEN DID THE FIRST CATS LIVE?

The first known cats lived 35 million years ago. They were the ancestors of two feline families. One produced all today's cats (big and small), the other was the saber-toothed family. The last saber-toothed tiger died out several millennia ago.

WHERE DO BIG CATS LIVE?

Mostly in Africa, but also in Asia and the Americas. Both African and Asian lions are at risk. There are even some medium-sized cats in Europe.

WHICH SPEEDY ANIMAL IS ENDANGERED?

The cheetah. It can run up to 62 mph. It can't keep up its speed over a long distance, but runs this fast in short bursts. Both the African and Indian cheetah are endangered.

Tigers are unusual cats because they like water.

ARE WHITE TIGERS AND SIBERIAN TIGERS EXTINCT?

Nearly. The Siberian tiger is paler than most other tigers, but still orange-brown in color. Truly white tigers are extremely rare. They are not a distinct species of tiger, as any species can produce a white tiger cub.

WHAT IS BIG AND LAZY?

The male lion is the biggest of the cat family, weighing about 528 lb. Despite his size, he does little work, leaving the hunting and killing of his food and the raising of cubs to the lioness. Lions can sleep for up to 20 hours a day. All lions are on the list of endangered animals.

WHICH BIG CATS ARE ENDANGERED?

Many big cats are endangered by hunters because of the beauty of their skin. Hunters can get rich selling the pelts (skins) of slaughtered big cats (such as the ocelot) to people who make fur coats. Some hunters still kill big cats for sport. Many big cats, such as the mountain lion, are also threatened with the loss of their habitat, which is destroyed by developers or by wars. The most endangered big cats are: mountain lion, tiger, snow leopard (also called an ounce), jaguar, ocelot, clouded leopard, iriomote, and cheetah.

IRIOMOTE CAT

TIGER

The iriomote looks very similar to a domestic cat.

DID GRAY SQUIRRELS KILL OFF RED SQUIRRELS?

No. The red squirrel was the only squirrel living in the UK until the gray squirrel was brought in from the USA. When red squirrels started to disappear in the UK, many people thought gray squirrels were killing them. But now scientists believe that the red squirrel was endangered by other predators, such as stoats, foxes, and eagles. A highly contagious disease also killed vast numbers of red squirrels in the first half of the 20th century. Gray squirrels are larger and more hardy than red squirrels, so have survived better.

WHICH SMALL MAMMALS ARE ENDANGERED?

Many small mammals, such as beavers in the USA and the red squirrel in Europe, are endangered because their habitat is being destroyed by humans developing land for building and farming. Others, such as weasels, are poisoned by dangerous chemicals used in industry and farming.

HOW SLEEPY ARE DORMICE?

Dormice are said to be very sleepy creatures, but in fact they don't sleep for long periods every day. Like many mammals (including squirrels and bears) they hibernate in winter. They go to sleep in October and wake up in April. They wake up from time to time in winter to eat food that they have stored up during the summer months. Dormice are endangered by pollution and pesticides.

Squirrels have very strong front paws for gripping their food.

HOW DO BEAVERS BUILD DAMS?

Beavers can cut down trees by biting through the trunk. Then they gnaw them into pieces and drag the logs to the water to build a dam. They lay the logs across each other and stop up any gaps with stones and mud. Beavers are severely endangered due to logging in Canada and North America.

GRAY SQUIRREL

ARE RATS RELATED TO SQUIRRELS?

Yes, they are both mammals called rodents. The rodent family (scientific name *Rodentia*) includes rats, mice, dormice, beavers, porcupines, and squirrels. Many of them, such as the lesser-toothed small rat and the common fieldmouse, are endangered. They all have strong front teeth (incisors), which they use to slice through vegetation, such as strong grasses and tree bark—and beavers even saw through tree trunks.

Like other mammals, rodents are warm-blooded and give birth to live young, which they feed with mother's milk.

WHERE DO OTTERS LIVE?

In Europe, Asia, and the Americas. Otters need unpolluted water and they live wherever the water is pure—in streams, canals, and lakes, in mountainous regions as well as in valleys. Many otters are endangered because habitat destruction has led them to starve or because they cannot find unpolluted water.

OTTER

RED SQUIRREL

Otters bark and chirp to communicate.

The Californian condor only lays one egg when it breeds and it doesn't breed until it is six years old.

CALIFORNIAN CONDORS

WHAT IS A BIRD OF PREY?

This group of birds includes eagles, falcons, hawks, and owls. Whereas most birds exist on a diet of small insects, nuts, and seeds, a bird of prey eats other birds and animals. Birds of prey have sharp, flexible talons (claws), used for grabbing their prey and for killing it. They also have hooked beaks for tearing and ripping at flesh. Because they are such beautiful creatures they are often hunted to be kept and trained as pets. The Californian condor is one huge bird of prey that is endangered.

The kakapo hides under tree roots and foliage during the day. At night it searches for food.

WHICH ARE THE BIGGEST AND SMALLEST BIRDS OF PREY?

The Andean condor is the largest bird of prey, with a wingspan of more than 10 feet. The smallest birds of prey are pygmy falcons. Some are only 6 inches long. Both of these birds are endangered by loss of habitat.

WHERE DO BUDGIES COME FROM?

Budgies, or budgerigars, are native to Australia, where flocks of them can be seen flying wild. Their name comes from an aboriginal word meaning colored bird. They are a member of the parakeet family—which also includes parrots, cockatiels, cockatoos, and lorikeets. Most wild budgerigars are green and yellow and they are at risk from hunters who shoot them as pests or capture them to sell to the pet trade.

WHAT IS THE WORLD'S RAREST BIRD?

Brazil's spix macaw. There is only one male left in the wild. Almost as rare is New Zealand's kakapo, of which there are only a few pairs left. Endangered birds include several birds of prey, shot as pests by farmers, and exotic birds, such as the flightless notornis, hunted by traders.

WHY ARE PEOPLE THE BIRDS' WORST ENEMIES?

People destroy birds' habitat by cutting down forests and draining marshland. A bird can die if it swallows a fishing hook or fishing line or garbage that would injure or choke it. People sometimes steal birds' eggs, but if they disturb or look in nests, parent birds and fledglings will leave their chicks to die. Exotic birds, such as parrots, pheasants, hummingbirds, eagles, and birds of paradise, are trapped to be sold as pets and often die while being transported. They are also killed for their beautiful feathers or to be stuffed.

ARE ANY BIRDS EXTINCT?

Yes. Some—such as the *Archaeopteryx*—died out with the dinosaurs. Others have been hunted to extinction more recently. The most famous extinct bird is the dodo, which lived on the island of Mauritius and was finally killed off by hungry sailors.

DO CROP PESTICIDES HARM BIRDS?

Yes. Birds that eat sprayed crops, such as budgerigars and lapwings, can die from poisoning. Farm chemicals also pollute rivers and marshes and destroy water birds, such as the Jamaica petrel and the crested ibis from Africa, and their habitat.

KAKAPO

HOW BIG IS THE BIGGEST WHALE?

The biggest whale is the blue whale which is now officially protected to prevent its extinction. It is the largest-known mammal ever to have lived. The average length of a female is 87 feet; males are shorter at about 80 feet. The biggest recorded blue whale measured 110 feet and weighed 176 tons.

WHY MUST WE SAVE THE WHALES?

The ecosystem of the seas is very delicate. Breaking one link in the food chain that goes all the way from the smallest microscopic creature to the biggest whale would have devastating effects. In 1986, the International Whaling Commission (IWC) announced a worldwide ban on whaling. Today it allows a small number of whales to be taken every year "for scientific reasons." Peoples like the Inuit, who have always depended on whaling, are allowed to continue whaling using traditional methods.

ARE KILLER WHALES KILLERS?

No. A killer whale, or orca, is unlikely to eat a person. They prefer to eat fish, other cetaceans, and seals. In fact they are in more danger from humans than vice versa. In New Zealand an orca once tried to eat a man diving near a colony of seals. The man was wearing a shiny black wetsuit and must have looked like a sleek, tasty sea lion. When the orca realized its mistake it spat the man out and he survived!

WHICH WHALE HAS A HORN LIKE A UNICORN?

The narwhal, which lives in waters around the Arctic and is almost extinct. The male narwhal has a horn or tusk, which is actually a very long tooth, made of ivory. Very occasionally a narwhal has two tusks. The myth of unicorns probably began when an explorer returned to Europe with a narwhal's tusk.

SPERM WHALE

A sperm whale can swim as much as half mile below the surface of the sea and hold its breath for around one hour.

HOW DO WHALES EAT?

All dolphins and porpoises and some whales have teeth. Other whales, such as the almost extinct blue whales, have baleen—this is a huge sieve, made up of hundreds of stiff blades of keratin, a type of protein like fingernails. Baleen whales sieve the microscopic shrimp-like creatures called krill with these tools. Toothed cetaceans, such as the endangered sperm whale, eat fish and sea mammals, such as seals, squid, and smaller cetaceans.

WHAT IS THE DIFFERENCE BETWEEN A DOLPHIN AND A PORPOISE?

They are quite hard to tell apart without examining their teeth! Dolphins have teeth shaped like cones, but porpoise's teeth are spade-shaped. Porpoises are usually smaller than dolphins and have more rounded bellies. The two groups often swim together and are extremely playful. There are endangered species within both groups, such as the vaquita porpoise and the Yangtze river dolphin.

Drift nets are lethal to dolphins, sharks, and many other sea creatures.

NARWHAL

DOLPHIN CAUGHT IN A DRIFT NET

HOW DO DRIFT NETS KILL DOLPHINS AND SHARKS?

Drift nets are enormous nets used for commercial fishing. They cover huge areas, often reaching right down to the seabed. The nets trap and kill many other sea creatures as well as fish—especially dolphins, porpoises, sharks, and turtles. Drift nets have been banned in most countries, but are still used illegally.

The narwhal's tusk is a very long tooth growing out from the upper jaw.

QUIZ
QUESTIONS

SECTION ONE
COLD-BLOODED CREATURES

1 What is the world's heaviest reptile?

2 What is the world's smallest reptile?

3 What is the gecko's favorite food?

4 What is the longest a snake can go without food?

5 What are egg caruncles for?

6 What are osteoderms?

7 Do lizards live in the Antarctic?

8 How may different kinds of lizard are there?

9 Which is the heaviest snake?

10 Do snakes have ears?

UP IN THE SKY

1 Which bird was worshipped by the ancient Aztecs?

2 Which bird lays the biggest egg?

3 Why do some birds have an egg tooth?

4 Which birds leave their young in other birds' nests?

5 How does a male frigate bird attract females?

6 What do male peacocks use their colorful tail feathers for?

7 Which bird eats the chicks of other birds?

8 Which Mauritian bird is now extinct?

9 Who was the Egyptian bird-god of wisdom?

10 What is another name for the peewit?

SECTION THREE

CREEPY CRAWLIES

1 Which spider's bite can cause heart failure and breathing problems?

2 How long are the largest millipedes?

3 Where does the dust mite like to live?

4 Why do some male wolf spiders "sing" to their mates?

5 How does the bola spider catch insects?

6 What causes mountain fever?

7 What produces honeydew?

8 Would ants attack humans?

9 How do bees know where to find good pollen sources?

10 What is the name of the "skin" that covers a snail's body and its shell?

SECTION FOUR

UNDERWATER WORLD

1 Whereabouts does the carpet shark live in the sea?

2 Which long, thin fish hides in seaweed?

3 How does the cuttlefish escape from its enemies?

4 Which crab doesn't have a shell of its own?

5 Is coral a plant or an animal?

6 Which fish lashes out with a sharp tail?

7 Which Australian jellyfish is deadly poisonous?

8 Can crocodiles ever live in the sea?

9 What is the largest animal on earth?

10 What is the smallest fish on earth?

SECTION FIVE

LIFE IN ARID LANDS

1 Which desert foxes use their large ears to keep cool?

2 What do ground squirrels use their tails for?

3 What protects a sand cat's feet from the hot desert sand?

4 What method does the king snake use to kill its prey?

5 How fast can a cheetah run?

6 Which snake can blind a human with its spit?

7 Where does the shingleback lizard live?

8 What do budgerigars eat?

9 What is special about a camel's eyelids?

10 How does a male sandgrouse bring water to its chicks?

KINGS OF THE JUNGLE

1   What is the word used to describe creatures that only come out at night?

2   What do termites use to glue their wooden towers together?

3   Why do orangutans burp?

4   What does a leaf-tailed gecko try to look like?

5   How many types of poisonous snake are there?

6   What is it that makes the humming sound of a hummingbird?

7   What is the loudest insect in the rainforest?

8   Which is the rarest rainforest animal?

9   How many hours a day does the three-toed tree sloth sleep?

10 How many mountain gorillas are left in the wild?

SECTION SEVEN
LIFE IN THE FROZEN WASTES

1 Which gray bear hibernates in winter?

2 Why do baby seals have white fur?

3 How do caribou save energy when they travel?

4 Why do wolves howl?

5 What large mammals do polar bears like to eat?

6 Which sharks can be found in the Arctic?

7 What is special about the blood of the icefish?

8 What does the bearded seal use its beard for?

9 What do Adelie penguins make their nests with?

10 How do Sandhill cranes attract a mate?

SECTION EIGHT
VANISHING LIFE

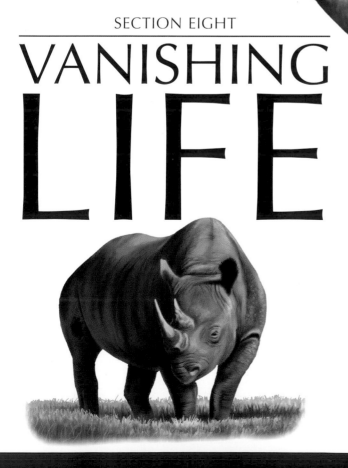

1 What are mature male gorillas called?

2 What term is used to describe animals who share similarities with humans?

3 Why did wolves become extinct in Britain?

4 Why are giant pandas in danger?

5 Where does the Kodiak bear live?

6 Which are bigger? Porpoises or dolphins?

7 How many species of rhino are there?

8 Which is the biggest member of the cat family?

9 Are squirrels rodents or mammals?

10 What does omnivorous mean?

QUIZ
ANSWERS

COLD-BLOODED CREATURES
1 The saltwater crocodile
2 The dwarf gecko
3 Flies
4 Two years
5 Baby reptiles use them to break out of their egg when they hatch
6 Scales on a crocodile's body
7 No
8 At least 2,500
9 The anaconda
10 No

UP IN THE SKY
1 The queztal
2 An ostrich
3 To break out of the egg when they hatch
4 The cuckoo
5 It inflates a red throat pouch
6 To attract mates and defend their territory
7 The jay
8 The dodo
9 Thoth
10 Lapwing

CREEPY-CRAWLIES
1 The Australian Sydney funnel-web spider
2 11 inches
3 In beds and mattresses
4 To distract them and try to save themselves from being eaten
5 It lets down a silk line with a sticky blob on the end and swings it around to catch passing insects
6 The rickettsia
7 Aphids
8 Yes
9 Other bees show them by their movements in a special dance
10 The mantle

UNDERWATER WORLD
1 On the seabed
2 The pipe fish
3 It produces a cloud of ink to confuse them and jets away
4 The hermit crab
5 An animal
6 The surgeonfish
7 The sea wasp jellyfish
8 Yes
9 The blue whale
10 The dwarf goby

LIFE IN ARID LANDS
1 The fennec fox and the kit fox
2 To shade themselves from the sun
3 Hair
4 Suffocation
5 62 mph
6 The red cobra
7 Australia
8 Seeds
9 They are thin enough to see through if the camel has to shut its eyes
10 It carries it on its feathers

KINGS OF THE JUNGLE
1 Nocturnal
2 Spit
3 To scare other males away from their territory
4 A woody bump
5 Around 400
6 The rapid beating of its wings as it hovers
7 The cicada
8 Golden lion tamarin
9 18
10 There are said to be under 40,000

LIFE IN THE FROZEN WASTES
1 The grizzly bear
2 To help to hide them from predators while they are on the ice
3 Each deer treads in the footsteps of the animal in front
4 To communicate with each other and to warn away rival wolves
5 Ringed seals
6 Greenland sharks
7 It contains no red cells
8 To feel for shellfish on the seabed
9 Pebbles
10 They perform "dances"

VANISHING LIFE
1 Silverbacks
2 Anthropoids
3 Because the forests were cut down, destroying their habitat
4 Because of the shortage of bamboo
5 In Alaska
6 Dolphins
7 Five: white, black, Sumatran, Javan, and Indian
8 The male lion
9 Rodents
10 If something is omnivorous, it eats both meat and plants

INDEX